GUDH ELF AND BADH ELF - BOOK 1

A PICTURE OF ELF

BY ROBIN PAUC

Copyright

First published in Great Britain in 2014

by Tinsley House Publications,

Tinsley House,

Main Road,

East Boldre,

Hampshire. SO42 7WT.

Illustrations Des Campbell

ISBN 978-1500721886

GUDH ELF AND BADH ELF

CONTENTS

Official Map of Elfland 2014
Seaview Sands
Brook
Isle of Widget
Orcborne Hse
East Tiddleton
Ventnoir
Old Port
Winkleton
West End
Winkle Inn
Orclando
The Great Forest of Orc
Funny Folk Farm Theme Park
The Tiddle
Tiddleton on Sea
Tiddley House
The Turf-cutter's Arms
Tiddleton
Trumpington
Port Elf
Boar's Head
West Lands
Orcland
Southlands
Spritely Minster
Ashton
New Forest of the South-lands
The Sidne
Gobham County
Tiddley Trumper
Much Trumping
The Piddle
Elfton
Tea room
Forests of the Northlands
Far North-lands
Elfex
Follywood
Eastlands
Fairy Down Meadow Adventure Park
Sandy Bottom
East End
Reekin
The Burping Bog
Wizardton
Northlands
Windy Bottom
Craicton on Sea
N
The Hooley Land
Trolland
Craicoff

1 GUDH ELF AND BADH ELF

Once upon a time, in a land not far from where you are right now, lived a little boy called Badh Elf. Well actually, he wasn't that little, as he was very fond of his food, and I do mean *very* fond of his food.

First thing in the morning, even before he was properly awake and while he was still rubbing his eyes, Badh was already thinking about breakfast. Cocoa Plops, toast with jam, chocolate biscuits and, if he was very lucky, pancakes dripping with syrup.

As far as Badh was concerned, there was only one good thing about going to school, and that was stopping off at the sweet shop on the way to stock up on sweets, chocolates, crisps and biscuits to keep him going until lunchtime.

Once in school, Badh could not keep still. It was as though all that food and all those sweets were driving him crazy. In the classroom, he would run about, and when his teacher spoke, he would shout out. He just couldn't keep still, let alone listen to his teacher and do his work.

In the playground, Badh didn't play because he had all those crisps and biscuits to eat, and anyway, why would he want to run around? On the odd occasion when he did join in with the other children, he usually ended up in trouble. Badh didn't know his own strength and would often be too rough, or if having a bad day, he would lash out at other children. Twice, in the past, when he had been told off by his teacher, he had even hit her.

When Badh wasn't running about or shouting out, he would fidget. The ants in his pants would make him fidget more and more as it grew closer to lunchtime. The thought of all that food just sitting there waiting for him was almost too much to bear.

Badh had a very big school bag. In fact it was ginormous. It had to be, to hold his lunch box. His lunch box was so big, that once it was in his bag, nothing else would fit in. There was certainly no place for boring things like books or coloured pencils, which he might need in class.

When the school bell rang at lunchtime, Badh would head straight for his school bag and the feast that it contained. There would be jam sandwiches, a chocolate muffin, crisps, cheese strings, sweets and, buried under all of this, a giant chocolate bar.

After lunch, Badh often didn't feel too well. Usually this passed, and

gradually he would get back to being his very noisy, very active and very annoying self. All this noise and activity not only stopped Badh from learning anything, but meant the whole class suffered too.

Sometimes, and it was usually on a Monday after a very busy weekend of eating everything in sight, Badh would have a tummy ache. When this happened, he would sit on the toilet for ages. Unfortunately, this often wouldn't help, and he didn't go, if you know what I mean, for days.

As Badh wasn't very good with his hands, and he was allergic to toilet paper and soap, quite often, when he couldn't go, his pants would become very smelly. Whenever this happened his mother would have to give him some very nasty medicine.

There was really only one good thing about school, and that was going home. When the school bell rang, Badh would stop whatever he was doing, including listening, and head for the school gate. He would drag his huge, empty bag behind him, usually forgetting to collect his coat, or hat, or even the letter his teacher had told him to give to his mummy.

Most days, after school, Badh and his mother would go to McDonkey's for tea. Sometimes this would be straight away, but on very special days it would be a bit later, when dad would join them for a "blow-out" as he called it. Either way, from the moment he left the school gate behind, Badh could think of nothing else but a Double Plopper giant burger, large fries, and his favourite cola.

On the special days when his dad would join them, they would end the meal with the biggest ice-cream on the menu covered with chocolate chips, brightly coloured sweets, strawberry sauce and hundreds-and-thousands. This often required another bucket of cola to help wash it down. Then Badh would wipe his very greasy, sticky hands on his shirt.

Sometimes, the journey home included a stop for Badh to be sick. It was always a time when various parts of Badh's and Badh's parents' bodies would make some very rude noises. Always, when they got home, Badh would have to lie down. Not because he was tired, but because he was pogged – fit to burst.

As bedtime approached, you would think that Badh would be getting tired and slowing down, but no. The nearer it got to bedtime, the more active Badh became. He would run, shout, scream, and if anyone tried to get him to go to bed, oh dear. Badh had been known to kick, punch, bite and scratch both his mummy and his daddy. Bedtime was never a happy time.

On the other side of Wizardton, far from Gremlin Close where Badh lived, there was another little boy called Gudh Elf. He lived with his parents and his little sister in Fairy Tale Crescent. No two boys could be as different as Badh and Gudh. Badh was very overweight, while Gudh was slim. Badh was often a little dirty, to say the least, while Gudh was always clean and very smart. Badh hated school and sports, while Gudh loved school and was brilliant at sports. Everybody wanted to be Gudh's friend, while only two, equally naughty boys would have anything to do with Badh.

Every morning, as soon as the birds started singing, Gudh would get himself up, clean his teeth, wash and dress. With this done, he would sit quietly in his favourite window seat and read a book, watch the birds on the bird table or practice his spellings while he waited for his mother to call him for breakfast.

Gudh's mother always said that breakfast was the most important meal of the day. As it was at least twelve hours since the last meal, she said it was very important to have a proper cooked breakfast. Although he loved her scrambled eggs on toast and her homemade fruit salad, her fishcakes with baked beans were his favourite.

Each morning, before setting off for school, Gudh's mother would make sure he had put his books, pencils, packed lunch and water bottle in his school bag. Whenever possible, they walked to school, as his mother said that a little bit of exercise in the morning got the brain ready for work.

They usually arrived at the school in good time and, if it was not raining, Gudh would hang his coat and bag on his peg before heading off to the playground to play football with his friends. Once the bell rang, Gudh would walk with his friends to the classroom to start work for the day.
In class, Gudh always listened to his teacher and worked quietly, trying to do his best. When the bell went for break, he would go to his peg, get an apple from his bag, and have a good drink of water. Then he would head off to play. His mother had told him that it was very important to drink lots of water in order to stay hydrated (or some big word like that).

After he had eaten his apple, had a good drink of water and a bit of a kick-about with his friends, Gudh was ready to settle down in his classroom and work until lunch time. Sometimes the work was a bit tricky, and every now and then he had to put his hand up and ask for help. However, he really enjoyed learning to read, write and do his sums. He really wanted to be a vet like his father, so he knew he had to work hard and learn as much as he could.

Lunchtimes were really special, as his mother always gave him a really good lunch, and it meant he could sit with his friends and talk about football, kite flying and what they were going to do at the weekend. Every time Gudh opened his lunch box, he thought how lucky he was to have a mummy who took time to make him really healthy sandwiches or wraps, chop up cucumber or carrots and always put in several pieces of fruit.

Once Gudh had eaten his lunch, chatted to his friends, been to the loo and washed his hands, it was time for another kick-around in the playground before going back into class. Gudh always found that the afternoons flew by, and before he knew it, his teacher would be telling the class to put their things away and line up.

On Mondays, his mother would take him swimming. On Wednesdays, it was tennis, and on Fridays and Saturdays, his father would take him to football practice, or a match. Every day after school, his mother would bring him a snack to eat. Some days it would be carrot sticks with a homemade dip, on others, a tub of mixed fruit. On a Friday and on Sunday, his father would give Gudh and his sister a little bar of chocolate as a special treat.

Once home, while Gudh played with his sister, his mother would busy herself preparing and cooking a delicious meal for the family. Gudh and his sister would often help their mother to get things ready for supper and always put the knives, forks, spoons, glasses and a big jug of water on the table ready for when their father would return from work and they could sit down to eat.

Once the meal was over, it was time for Gudh to have a bath before putting on his pyjamas and joining his sister and parents for family time. For the next half an hour or so, they would talk about what they had done during the day. Just before bedtime, Gudh's father would read three or four pages of a really good book to them. After kisses and cuddles all round, Gudh would head for his bed, and sometimes he would be fast asleep before his mother came up to tuck him in.

Friday the 29th of February was not a good day for Badh. It is just as well that such days don't happen too often. First of all, he was caught taking some money out of his mother's purse, which of course, is a very naughty thing to do. Because of this, she said she would not be taking him to the sweet shop on the way to school. This made Badh very angry, which he said was the reason he punched a little girl in his class before kicking his teacher. Oh dear.

Mrs Elf immediately had a telephone call from the Headmaster, telling her what had happened and asking her to come to the school straightaway. When she got to the school, Badh was in the Headmaster's office together with his teacher and another teacher who helped children if they couldn't read very well. The Headmaster said Badh should see a doctor and someone called a tricky cyclist, and that he would have to have some medicine if he was going to stay at the school. The teachers all nodded, and Mrs Elf cried.

Once home, Mrs Elf rang her husband and said he should come home straight away. Badh hid under his bed as he was sure something terrible was about to happen. And it did. Before too long, he could hear his father shouting and his mother crying yet again. Fortunately for Badh, he had been saving spare sweets and chocolates. He opened the two biscuit tins he kept under the bed, and tucked in.

Downstairs, Mrs Elf was still sobbing, while Mr Elf was walking up and down trying to think what to do next. Shouting at Badh wasn't going to help, so he had to think of something they could do that would help. Suddenly, a thought popped into his head – Avery Longbottom. Before you could say "Jack Flash", Mr Elf was on the phone and talking to his old friend, Avery.

Avery listened as Mr Elf talked at length, and that's a very long time, about Badh. He told him about the school; how he had hit other children; how he had kicked his teacher; and all the other things the Headmaster had said.

When at last Mr Elf stopped talking, Avery said "Is That My Child?"

Mr Elf really didn't know what Avery was talking about. So Avery explained about a book he had just read, which was all about children with problems like Badh.

Within two days, Mr and Mrs Elf had read the book and had made an appointment to see the man who had written it. Mr Elf would have to take a day off work, and they would all have to make the long journey to the clinic, but they thought it would certainly be worth doing. Badh was not so sure. He had heard his mother and father talking about what it said in the book, and he hated the man who had written it already.

On the long journey to the clinic, Badh was very quiet, which was not like him at all. He was not very happy, perhaps a little scared and secretly was planning what he could do to make the visit go horribly wrong. Maybe he could make himself be sick; he certainly wouldn't do as he was told, and if there was any chance at all, he was going to kick the man they were going to see.

When they got to see the man, he was in fact very nice, friendly and really funny. Badh had to try very hard to stay grumpy, and almost burst out laughing twice. The man asked Mrs Elf lots of questions, and then Badh about all sorts of things. Badh was having none of it and refused to speak. Mr Elf was getting very angry. He told Badh to behave himself and talk to the man. The man said that if Badh didn't want to speak, that was OK, and was very nice about the whole thing. It was at this point that Badh decided to hit the man, and knock his glasses off.

As the man put his glasses back on, he said that he wanted to do some tests. He asked Badh very nicely, but Badh refused to cooperate. Mr and Mrs Elf were very upset that Badh was being so naughty after they had travelled so far. The man said it didn't matter, and he explained that they could do the tests on another day. He then gave Mrs Elf some sheets of paper all about the vitamins, minerals, and oils that he wanted Badh to take. Badh thought the oils were to stop him from squeaking.

The man explained how the vitamins, minerals and oils were to help Badh's brain to grow properly. He then started talking about what Badh had been eating, and how there were too many bad fats, too many brightly coloured sweets, too many biscuits, crisps and cakes in Badh's diet. In fact, too much food. The man then told Mrs Elf just what Badh was to eat each day, including lots of fruit and vegetables, which, of course, would be very good for his bowels (whatever they were).

For the next six weeks, Badh had a cooked breakfast, fruit for his break at school, one sandwich, some raw vegetables and fruit for lunch, and more fruit to eat on the way home. They didn't stop at the sweet shop any more, and they didn't go to McDonkey's for their tea. Each evening, Mrs Elf cooked a delicious meal with meat or fish and, what appeared to Badh to be a mountain of vegetables.

Every morning, Badh had to stand on his left leg and clean his teeth with his left hand for two minutes. If that wasn't bad enough, he then had to walk up and down three steps of the stairs with his eyes shut. He had to do these exercises three times a day, and since they had been to the clinic his father had been very strict with him and made sure he did do them.

Even though Badh moaned and protested every day about what he had to eat, and the fact that he was not allowed to have Double Ploppers any more, really, he was enjoying the change and feeling so much happier. By the time they had to go back to the clinic, Badh was so much calmer and happier, and he had only been in trouble at school on one occasion. And that wasn't his fault, if you believe what Badh said.

When they arrived at the clinic, Badh sat very still with his head down and waited for the man to come out of his room. The last time he was at the clinic, he had been very naughty and he wondered if the man was going to be angry. When the man came out to get them he called Badh "The Bard" and had him laughing in seconds. They did all the tests together, and the man gave Badh a special computer program to use at home to help to get his brain to work really well.

Mr and Mrs Elf and "The Bard", as he was now known, had to visit the clinic a few times, but from that first visit when he had been so very naughty, Bard just got better and better. He was a good boy in school, and in no time at all, he had learnt to read and write. He started to play football and go swimming twice a week, and at night he was out of the bath, dried, in his PJ's, and into bed before you could say "Jack Flash".

One Saturday, Bard and his mother went to the park so that he could fly his kite. When they got there, another boy, who looked very much like Bard, had his kite flying high already. In no time at all, the two boys were talking, as were their mothers who sat side-by-side on a park bench. This was the first time Bard and Gudh had met. It would be the beginning of a friendship that would last for many years to come.

2 THE RETURN OF BADH ELF

In a land where this world ends and at least a footstep within the realm of fantasy (so that would be at least past the Isle of Wight), lived a little boy called Badh Elf. Well I say, "little boy". In fact, little could not be further from the truth. The one thing Badh was known for was his lumps, bumps and bulges.

No matter where you looked, some part of his body was trying to escape from his clothes, which often caused panic, made girls scream and resulted in injury as his clothes, no longer able to hold him within, exploded.

On one occasion, Badh yawned, stretched and leant back, all at the same time, which caused his shirt and jacket to give up the fight, and sent a particularly large button flying through the air.

Not only was the button large and thick, but it travelled at an amazing rate of knots, and with deadly accuracy straight into Mrs Longbottom's right eye. The injury was so severe that Mrs

Longbottom was off work for the rest of the week. When she returned, she was wearing an eye patch, perhaps as a badge of honour, rather than out of necessity.

In those days, Badh was so bad, that he had no friends, would hit other children, and one day even kicked a teacher. Now, that is really bad, so he had to go and see the Headmaster. The Headmaster called his parents, who came to the school, which made his mother cry.

Things got so bad, that Badh was taken off to see a doctor who wagged his finger at him. It is really serious when a doctor does that. Badh had to stop eating junk food, take some supplements, whatever they are, and do some special exercises. Before you could say a very long sentence, Badh became "The Bard". Well, at least that is what the doctor called him, and the doctor told him it meant something like "smarty-pants".

Bard had been really good in school, helpful at home, and had made lots of friends. In fact, it was like he was a different boy until that day, that awful, dreadful day when, having found some money that had been left on the side at home, Bard had bought a great, big bag of very brightly coloured sweets.

He ate one, then another, then another and then, yet another. When they were all gone, he felt a little strange, and, having some money left over, decided that a large bottle of Cola was just what he needed to make him feel better. It didn't. He now felt very strange, upset, and very, very angry, and the world was about to find out just how angry he was.

On the way home, he tried to hit two children, but fortunately missed. He swore at an old lady and kicked over somebody's bike. Once home, when his mother asked him about the missing money, his anger knew no bounds. Furniture was knocked over, items flew around the room and the cat, sensing something terrible was about to happen, jumped out of the window.

Something terrible was about to happen, and would have done so, had it not been for his father entering the room just as Bard was about to throw a chair at his mother. With his father in hot pursuit, Bard flew up the stairs, and was already pulling off his clothes to get into his pyjamas, by the time his father entered his bedroom.

I won't tell you how angry his father was, for fear of frightening you. It was so scary, Bard fell silent, got into bed and started crying. Something had to be done. After comforting his wife, and letting the cat back in, Mr Elf was on the phone to the clinic to book an urgent appointment to see the doctor.

The next morning, things did not get off to a good start. Bard woke early and crept downstairs. Once in the kitchen, he started searching the fridge, cupboards and draws for anything that might be sweet. Having found half a bar of chocolate, eleven biscuits, a small pot of jam, two cereal bars and half a bottle of cherry flavour cough medicine, he returned to his room.

Here, he again started searching, but this time for money. By the time the search was over, he had enough money hidden in his school bag to buy enough sweets for him and the entire Elfland army. Now came the tricky bit. Somehow, Bard needed to get past his parents and out of the house. To do this, he decided it would be best if he kept very quiet, didn't mention anything about last night, and kept his fingers crossed.

Having washed and dressed, he headed downstairs, trying to make out that everything in the world was fine, and that nothing had ever happened. Unfortunately, the chair that now had a leg missing, the dent in the wall where the vase had struck, and the stain on the carpet, rather suggested that something had happened, something that could not be brushed under the carpet, so to speak.

When his mother entered the room, Bard's worst fears were realised, as the story of the previous night was written all over her face in tears. He tried to be nice, said he wasn't feeling too good and didn't fancy any breakfast. This last bit was true. Bard had already consumed lots of the chocolate, biscuits and cough medicine and it was doing very strange things in his tummy.

At this point, he was hoping to slip out of the house and go straight to school. Well, straight to school via the sweet shop. His master plan was foiled when his mother told him that she would walk with him to school. He said she didn't need to, that he was alright, that he thought he might take his bike, but she was having none of it.

As he reluctantly walked at her side, Bard worked on plan B, which would, of course, require leaving school at some point. As they passed the sweet shop, the smell of sweets passed up his nose and entered his brain. Now he knew for sure that he had to fill his every pocket, and his school bag, with sweets, more sweets, and even more sweets.

To escape from school would require a very cunning plan, and a little help. Bard's friend Randelf was sure to help, so Bard told him to tell his teacher that Bard had been taken very ill with dire-rear, and had to see Matron. While Randelf explained to Mrs Longbottom why Bard was missing from class, Bard slipped out of school and headed for the sweet shop, then the cake shop, and finally, the corner shop to top up on more fizzy pop.

Unfortunately, Randelf could not help himself, and in his excitement at being part of the cunning plan B, went a little over the top. He told Mrs Longbottom that, not only did Bard have dire-rear, but that it was so bad

Matron had placed him in a black plastic waste bag, which she had then taped around his waist, before he had been collected by his mother.

This was when the cunning plan B fell apart. Mrs Longbottom was so concerned about Bard's serious condition, that she set the class some work, and then hurried off to speak with Matron.

Oh dear. Mrs Longbottom spoke to Matron, who then spoke to the Headmaster, who then rang Bard's mother. Bard's mother rang his father, who left work to join her in the search of Bard, and the day took a turn for the worse for him. As they drove around the town, Mrs Elf was sobbing and Mr Elf was fuming, while in the park Bard sat surrounded by cakes, chocolate, sweets, fizzy pop, biscuits, and even more brightly coloured sweets. Could any boy be happier?

The park was the last place that Mr and Mrs Elf decided to look. By this time, the cakes, chocolate, biscuits, fizzy pop and most of the sweets had been hurriedly placed in his mouth, lovingly chewed and swallowed. It was at this point that two very, very bad things happened.

Firstly, Bard's tummy started making strange movements, causing him to make some very rude noises. This was followed by a pain in his tummy that was so bad, it made him think of every bad disease he had ever heard of. Secondly, while in this terrible state of pain, and while producing even more rude noises, he was spotted by his parents.

So concerned were his parents that they took him immediately to the hospital, where he was seen by two doctors, three nurses, two cleaning ladies and seven porters. In fact, he only needed to be seen by one doctor, but all the others came to take a look as news spread around the hospital of Bard's condition. Even the man from the ticket booth in the car park came in, as he could hear such a variety of rude noises over the sound of all the traffic.

After two hours, Bard was allowed to go home. Once indoors, it was bath and bed immediately, and of course, no supper. Bard hoped that he would drift off to sleep, but his tummy had other ideas. It kept him awake and running backwards and forwards to and from the toilet for most of the night. As if that was not bad enough, he could hear his parents downstairs talking about him, and about how things had to change.

In the morning, even though he told his parents he was too ill to move, let alone travel, he was taken shouting and protesting to see the doctor he had seen all that time ago. In the car, on the long journey, he wondered what lies he could tell, and what terrible things were about to happen to him. He need not have worried, as the doctor was calm and friendly at first, before suggesting that he deserved fifty lashes with a wet lettuce leaf for such bad behaviour. Even Bard could not help but raise a smile.

The doctor talked to his parents at length, and that's a very long time, before turning to Bard and giving him a warm, wide smile. At first, Mrs Elf had stuck to what the doctor had said, and given Bard a very healthy diet, fish oils, vitamins and minerals.

However, over the months, she had let things slip. She had allowed Bard to have Cocoa Plops for breakfast, and gradually more and more sweet things. She had also forgotten to order more fish oils and minerals, and now Bard's brain was screaming for sugar. Bard was not sure what "A diction" was, but the doctor said he had one.

On the journey home, Mrs Elf read the list of instructions the doctor had given her, and what made it worse was that she read them out loud. Taking the fish oils and minerals was not too bad, but the bit about no cereals, no biscuits, no crisps, no fizzy pop, and no sweets just sounded like no life at all. Mr Elf drove and nodded. Oh dear. Bard felt that things were not going to be too much fun and, when they stopped to eat at a service station, his worst fears appeared in front of him, looking very much like a salad.

That night Bard hoped he would be able to sleep, but his mind kept teasing him with thoughts of puddings, and ice-cream with chocolate sauce. When the thoughts left him for a moment, the idea of a life without fizzy pop and cakes tormented him. All night, or so it seemed, he was awake, and unable to think of anything, except how terrible his life would become, deprived of all his favourite foods.

In the morning, things took a turn for the better, when his mother told him he was not going to school, and could stay in his room. He had to eat scrambled eggs on toast first, but this was worth it to get a day off school, and a chance to play in his room all day.

When he returned to his room, all his toys were gone, and there, on his bed, was a book written by the doctor they had seen the day before. His mother said he had to read three chapters, and then he would spend the rest of the day doing extra maths homework. In life, we sometimes have a bad day, but this was not just bad, it was a word that Bard could not say properly, a word that sounded like "cat an throw pig", and that is really bad.

That night, Bard slept like a log, and in the morning, he woke up feeling really happy. At least, he was happy, until his mother sat him in front of a plate of sausages and beans, fish oils, vitamins and minerals, and told him to eat up, and take all the pills.

He thought he had better do as he was told, and was rather hoping that if he was good, he might at least get his Nintendo back. It was not to be. More reading, more maths, handwriting practice, and capitals of the world were to occupy his entire day, and even when he got cramp in his hand, he was not allowed to stop.

After a week of home schooling, a strict diet, tablets and no toys, he was allowed to return to school under the strict supervision of Miss Payne, the Special Needs teacher. She wasn't called Payne without reason, as it seemed she knew what Bard was thinking before he did. She could tell when he was lying and knew every trick in the book. She was, as Bard said to himself, a complete pain.

Gradually, the diet and the pills started working, and Bard stopped thinking about the need for an endless supply of junk food. He started looking forward to the meals his mother made, didn't mind taking the tablets, and actually enjoyed going to school.

Of an evening, once his homework was done, he would play football with his mates. At the weekend, he would play happily at home, or visit places with his parents. None of the horrible things he imagined would happen to him happened, and life was good.

Two months later, his parents took him back to see the doctor. He was very pleased with Bard, and told him so. Mrs Elf told him about his diet and the fish oils, vitamins and minerals, and the doctor told her how important it is for children like Bard, who like sweet things, to have the minerals.

He explained about a little bit of the brain that can get to like sugar too much. If children have a healthy diet and take vitamins and minerals, like zinc and magnesium, their brains can recover. Mrs Elf said she would make sure that she kept to the rules this time. The doctor smiled, and Bard found himself smiling too.

From that day on, Bard never looked back. He never ate junk food, always took his tablets and, in fact, went on to help other children who had problems reading, writing or keeping still.

Well done Bard!

3 THE BARD COMIC

It was Saturday morning in Elfland, and probably most other countries in the world, but not necessarily so. Saturday meant no school, not having to get up at the crack of dawn, and most importantly, football. Ever since Bard could remember, he had dreamt of playing for Elfield United. At one time, probably having had too much fizzy pop, he had considered Ashtown Villa, but had decided against it when their losing streak went into freefall.

Even as Bard began to wake up from his slumbers, he was still dreaming of scoring the winning goal and running around the pitch like a headless chicken, his shirt pulled up over his head. Oh dear. Once Bard was very near to being fully awake, a sound entered his ears, or at least one of them, and his heart sank. He climbed out of bed, tripped over the clothes that he had left on the floor, stubbed his toe on the bed leg, and, still hopping around in a considerable amount of pain, eventually pulled the curtains aside.

The wind was howling, causing tree branches to whip back and forth. More importantly, it wasn't just raining, it was pouring. As every boy knows, you can still dribble in drizzle and miss in the mist, but pouring is just boring.

The pitch would be water-logged, Elf and Safety would be the excuse, and the match would be cancelled. With his big toe still throbbing, Bard hobbled off to the bathroom and got washed and dressed very grumpily, in readiness for a thoroughly boring day ahead.

The good thing about going downstairs any day, even on a day such as this, when, not only is it pouring with rain but your big toe now feels as though it is going to explode, is the smell of sizzling sausages, crispy bacon and sunny-side up eggs. Not so this morning. Surely, things could not get any worse? No football, terminal toe pain and now, no breakfast.

"Come on Bard," said his father, "I decided to give your mother the morning off. We are going out for the Full Elfish."

Bard did not need to be told twice. He managed an amazing feat of multitasking in putting on his shoes, coat and hat, while hobbling towards the car.

With a Full Elfish, and two glasses of pure apple juice inside him, Bard was beginning to think that the world was a better place. But the wind was still making the trees bend this way and that, and the rain was still - yes you've guessed it - pouring down.

Having passed through the now flooded roads, and returned home, the only thing to look forward to was a boring day with nothing to do. The suggestion by his mother that he might start his homework, did nothing to improve Bard's mood of doom and gloom. In fact, strangely enough, it made the pain in his toe return with a vengeance.

Seeing the look on his face, a look that only very bored boys with no football can muster, Bard's father suggested that Bard should fetch the amazing pen and pencil set Bard had received for his birthday and, as yet, hadn't used, and do some drawing at the dining room table. Initially, this did no more than cause Bard to make an "I'm bored" grunt. However, it obviously triggered the "better-than-nothing" response, as, after a little while, Bard limped off to find the pen and pencil box. Carrying the box while having to hop was never going to be easy. When Bard reached the dining room table, and stubbed the same toe again, it was almost too much to bear.

Had he been an adult, Bard would probably have said one of those very rude words that adults say when they hit their thumb with a hammer, or burn themselves when getting something very hot out of the oven. But Bard was not an adult and so he did what boys in the worst pain ever do; he screamed and shouted, and then kicked the table, which, of course, only made things worse. Bard's mother did what she could to comfort him.

As every mother knows, when words of comfort are not enough, distraction is required. Mrs Elf suggested that Bard should start his colouring, and make a nice picture. Of course, she reminded him, he could always start his homework instead. The mention of homework on a Saturday - a Saturday when it was (still) pouring with rain - was enough to cause Bard to open his wooden box of pens and pencils. They were all arranged neatly on shelves that rose up as he opened the box. Bard put pens and pencils to paper.

Whether it was real enjoyment, or a cunning plan to avoid doing any homework on a Saturday when it refused to stop raining, Bard spent the entire day drawing, and only stopped briefly for a somewhat late, and light lunch. By the time it got round to supper, the project was complete, and the rain had stopped (too late!). Bard put away all his pens and pencils, tidied away all the pads of paper, rulers and his geometry set, and started laying the table in readiness for the evening meal. This done, he proudly positioned The Bard Comic in the centre of the table in such a way that his parents would not be able to miss it.

They did not miss it, and would have let their food go cold, were it not for this being considered to be very poor table manners. Poor manners are only considered as being acceptable under very exceptional circumstances, whatever they are. Everyone ate their dinner and then Mum looked at the comic before passing it to dad, and then asked that he should pass it back to her, as she wanted to read again the story on page three.

Bard was so pleased with himself that he forgot all about his terminal toe pain for a full twenty minutes. His parents took the comic through into the sitting room, to look at it again while sitting in front of the fire, which of course is one of the best places to look at a quality comic.

All the excitement of the day did not, in any way, replace the need that a boy has to score goals, but it did put an idea in Bard's head. That idea was to see The Bard Comic become a regular monthly offering which would be printed and handed out at his school. Now, when you are a great writer (and obviously Bard was a great writer, because his mother had said so), you need to keep producing good quality work. When you are a boy, and you have so many other, very important things to do in your life, like scoring goals, playing conkers (still allowed in Elfland under strict Elf and Safety rules and regulations), not to mention eating, which all growing boys have to do, finding time to write is not easy.

Being a smart young man, and perhaps because when he was younger, he had had an amazing ability to do as little as possible unless it involved him having fun, Bard remembered a word his father had used and decided to put it to good use. The word was "deli-plate" or something like that, which basically means getting other people to do all the hard work, while making sure you get all the praise. It certainly seemed like a good idea to Bard, and so he decided to be the person who did the least amount of work, and the most deli-plating. With this in mind, he asked his mother very nicely, on a day when she was humming–always a good sign in mothers–if she could give him a recipe for his healthy eating page in the comic.

Fortunately for Bard, his mother thought it was a very good idea, and said she would let the editor–Bard the deli-plater that is–have two healthy recipes by the end of the day. While she busied herself in the kitchen, Bard's mother started thinking about what might be suitable for the comic. Before long, she had decided on her magic scrambled eggs with smoked salmon as a healthy breakfast, and Rat stew, which was great for children as it contained loads of vegetables.

Her scrambled eggs, while being delicious, were not in fact magic, but relied upon the tiniest drop of cooking oil being added to the beaten eggs the very second they were added to the warm butter in the saucepan. This technique caused the eggs to cook more slowly, making them wonderfully creamy and totally lump free. Magic!

Mrs Elf's recipe for Rat stew had been " borrowed" (and that is putting it politely) from someone else's book. But Mrs Elf had made it her own. Fortunately, it did not contain one single rat, and was only called Rat stew, because very few people could spell the dish's long, foreign name. Rat stew was a mixture of wonderful vegetables that were prepared separately and then blended together, so that the flavours mingled and the whole thing became a meal fit for an elf king. The first time Bard had it, he had eaten all the vegetables, but left the meat, fearing that it might be a very large fillet

of rat. He only ate it after his mother and father assured him that it was, in fact, chicken.

Having successfully conned (which was, in Bard's mind, another word for "convinced") his mother into writing a page for the next edition of his comic, Bard decided to con Miss Payne to write something about helping children to read. After all, Miss Payne was a teacher with special training in helping such children. Miss Payne, even though her name would not suggest it, was usually very cheery, often humming, and always ready to help. With this in mind, Bard took the earliest opportunity to con her, and was delighted when she agreed to write about eye problems in children struggling to read.

Everything in the world of deli-plating was going so well, Bard thought he would take it to a whole new level. He would not only con more adults into providing items for the comic, but he would ask the Headmaster if the best painting or story by a child in the school could be included each month in the comic. Now, getting your mum to help is one thing, but asking to see your Headmaster takes a huge amount of courage, and an amazing ability to control your bodily functions.

On the way to the headmaster's office, at precisely 3.35pm, Bard remembered the last time he had had to visit the Headmaster. It had been after the whole dire-rear business. Bard recalled walking the green mile; he remembered losing control of his limbs, so that they twitched uncontrollably, and more unfortunately, losing control of his bottom so that it made a very rude noise with each step that he took. Not so today. Bard was trying hard to remain focused, and only allowing himself to think about how to get Mr Whackham, the headmaster, to help him with his comic.

He need not have worried. Not only was Mr Whackham pleased to see Bard, he thought the whole idea of the comic was brilliant, and he was more than happy to help. He even suggested getting the ladies in the school office to help with the printing and copying, not to mention the all-important distribution of the finished comic among the children. Now that is what you call serious deli-plating when you can not only con Mr Whackham, but get him to do even more deli-plating.

On his way back down the very long, narrow, green corridor, Bard felt extremely proud of himself. In fact, he felt that he was a bit of a hero, like the time he'd scored the winning goal in the last three minutes of extra time for Elfield United, making him man of the match (even though this had only been a dream, a very vivid dream, but a dream nevertheless). When he told his mother about the meeting with Mr Whackham and how the ladies in the office were going to help, his mother was overjoyed, shed a little tear of happiness, and suggested a well-deserved ice cream on the way home. Could life be any better for a boy?

The next three weeks were a busy time for Bard, as he worked on designing the cover of the comic, collected the recipes, stories and pictures, and decided where they should be in the comic. He also had a fair amount of writing to do himself, but not nearly as much as it would have been without that stroke of genius that saw him getting others involved in the production of the comic. Yes, being an editor was really a very good job, and before he knew it, Bard was handing over the finished comic to the nice lady in the school office who had always called him "My love" and patted him on the head.

The first official edition of The Bard Comic was a huge success. It was mentioned in morning assembly, talked about in class by Miss Payne, and caused great excitement when it was handed out to all the children.

When it was time to go home, Bard watched as all the children left the school with his comic in their hands, or sticking out of their satchels or pockets. No one could have been more proud of their son that day than Mrs Elf, and yes, yet again she shed a tear of joy. This caused Bard to remark, "Mother! This is getting embarrassing!"

That very evening, while his father was admiring the first printed edition of The Bard Comic, Bard remembered another word his father had used. The word sounded like an "enter-printer", and meant someone who was good at thinking up not only cunning plans and good ideas as Bard was, but also getting other people to do most of the work while still keeping most of the money. This idea appealed to Bard, and he decided there and then to become an enter-printer, and thereby Elfland's first ever millionaire.

That night in bed, all snuggled up, Bard's mind thought of all the wonderful things he would do when he was a very rich businessman. He would buy a big, new house for himself and his parents, and maybe, his very own football team one day. Bard knew, for a fact, that a lady who wrote cookery books had a football team, so surely a great enter-printer like him could have one too.

In the morning he was up, washed and dressed in a flash, and downstairs even before his mother had started cooking the breakfast. When his father appeared in the kitchen, Bard asked him if he could have his old briefcase. His father said he could, but asked Bard why he needed it. Clearly, his father had no idea about what an enter-printer needs if he is to do his job properly.

In school, Bard found that the work seemed easier, the time passed more quickly, and he felt very pleased with himself. At first, he could not

Perfict example of an Enter-printer, like Alan Sugary.

understand why this should be, but then all of a sudden it dawned on him: now he was an enter-printer and soon-to-be millionaire, he knew why he had to work hard in school. All of a sudden he had a reason to study, and if you are going to walk around with a very big briefcase, you really do need to be smart.

During the days that followed, Bard could not believe just how well things were going. In fact, he was already thinking about the possible changes he would make at Elfield United when he bought the club, and whether the FA would allow ogres to play if he promised they would not eat the ball boys. It was at this very moment in time that a brick wall ran into him, sending him and his briefcase flying.

The brick wall in question was Bradelf, a boy who was known throughout the school, town and probably the whole of Elfdom for three things. Firstly, he was big, and I do mean *big.* Secondly, he had a very bad temper, and thirdly, he had even more of a bad temper when he was hungry.

Once, or so it was said, he sat on a much smaller elf, causing him to make a sound just like a whoopee-cushion. Afterwards the elf had to spend the entire day with matron. And, after all that, would you believe, Bradelf did not even say he was sorry?

Not having the back-up of the entire Elfland army, Bard decided cowardice

was the best plan of action and played dead until Bradelf had scattered a group of small children, and charged through the swing doors almost taking them with him. Only at this point did Bard feel it was safe to get up and try to look like a self-made millionaire, even if he was covered in dust and two cobwebs.

That evening, Bard asked his mother about when he was bad, rude and angry all the time, and wondered if Bradelf would be happier if he too went to see the doctor who had helped him so much. At first, she said that she would not wish Bradelf on anybody, but then stopped and thought about whether anything could be done to help.

Later that evening, Bard's mother had a quiet talk with her husband. (That is what grownups do when they have something important to talk about.) She told him about what Bard had said, and wondered what could be done and how. Mr Elf had got on very well with Bard's doctor, and suggested calling him in the morning to get his advice.

In the morning, that is just what Mr Elf did, and the doctor said that providing he could rule out Ogreism, Trollism and Thrummy-cap syndrome, he was sure he could help the boy. Now came the tricky bit, for somehow they had to tell Bradelf's parents what the doctor had said, and try to get some help for the boy before it was too late.

Often, when you have a tricky situation such as this, it is just a matter of waiting for the perfect opportunity, and that happened at 3.33pm precisely. While waiting at the school gate for Bard to appear, Bradelf's mother ended up standing right next to Mrs Elf, and they exchanged smiles as you do on these occasions.

What happened next could not have been planned or even imagined. In the middle of the packed playground Bradelf appeared, scattering children in all directions and causing utter mayhem. Now, mayhem has nothing to do with a month of the year, because it has been known to occur in September.

But occur it did and it was not a pretty sight.

Bradelf's mother gripped Mrs Elf's arm, placed a hand over her mouth, and let out a muffled cry. While every teacher in the school, the caretaker and a passing policeman, tried to sort out the carnage in the playground (which resulted in the policeman's hat being knocked off), Mrs Elf comforted Bradelf's mother.

While order was restored in the playground, and matron and several teachers applied sticky plasters to numerous injured children (and a few others that just liked having a plaster on), the two woman talked. By the time the injured, pretend injured and uninjured children had been attended to and shepherded away by their parents, the two women had arranged to meet the following morning for a cup of tea.

Well, it was not a cup of tea, or a pot for that matter, but at least two pots and several biscuits. After a very, very long talk, some tears, and a few carefully chosen words, Bradelf's mother knew exactly what she had to do. Once home, she rang the doctor, booked an appointment, and then called her husband and told him what the plan was.

Although Bradelf's father immediately suffered an acute pain in his wallet (and that is something only a husband can feel), he knew something had to be done, and arranged to take a day off work in order to drive his wife and son all the way to the clinic. It was to be a journey none of them would forget easily, and the turning point in Bradelf's life.

While driving the long way to the clinic, Bradelf's father wished there was a short way, as Bradelf was kicking-off in the back, his mother was crying in the front, and he was wondering what happens to the father of a child that throws a doctor out of the window and then wrecks his office.

As it happened, he need not have worried. Although Bradelf tried his best to look incredibly big and scary, at the first mention of a blood test he fainted, and was putty in the doctor's hands thereafter. The Good Doctor, who was far too kind to even suggest Bradelf was a big girl's blouse, took the opportunity to examine Bradelf, while he was calm.

The doctor said some very nice things about Bradelf, and told his parents exactly what the problem was, and what could be done to help. He showed them the cherrybellbum, or something like that, on a model of a brain, and said this was why Bradelf was so clumsy. He then went on to explain about how something on the inside of his brain wasn't working too well, and that was why he was so active, and got very grumpy at times.

They all left the clinic feeling much happier than when they had arrived. Mum wasn't crying, dad was humming and Bradelf was just so pleased that someone knew what was happening in his brain, and even happier that he didn't have to have the blood tests. Overall, it had been a good day, and as the doctor had said, it was a fresh start.

The next morning, Bradelf was up early and downstairs in no time, as the smell of bacon wafted up the stairs. There was no cereal on the table or in the cupboard, as his mother had put it in the rubbish bin. Instead, there were eggs and bacon and toast. Even though he was a bit miffed about the lack of Coco Plops, Bradelf had to admit to himself that this was a pretty good start to the day, and on top of that, no school.

Following the mayhem in the playground, it was thought best if Bradelf stayed at home for a few days while the treatment took hold, and the children recovered from having seen a Bradelf in full flight. "What joy," thought Bradelf, "a cooked breakfast and no school, could a day be any better?" The answer was a very definite no.

Although Mr Whackham had thought it best if Bradelf stayed at home for a few days while the dust settled, so to speak, he had also thought it wise to supply him with some homework to be completed on a daily basis. Now some homework is bad enough, but when the stacked papers and books are nearly two feet tall, in Bradelf's mind that was close to child abuse.

The days passed, the homework was completed, his diet was changed, the supplements were taken, daily exercises for the cherrybellbum were done, and before Bradelf knew it, it was time to return to school. Small children do not forget such things as a Bradelf in full flight, and as he entered the school gate, they scattered in all directions.

Some children hid behind bushes, others behind the dustbins, and one very tall, thin boy hid behind a netball post, hoping beyond hope that he would not be spotted and thrown like a javelin far across the playing field. As it was, Bradelf walked slowly across the playground and entered the school. The children, and at least three teachers, came out of hiding.

In the school, Bard was in a little world of his own, thinking about the next edition of the comic, and not paying any attention as to what was walking down the corridor straight towards him. It was only when what could have been the shadow of an ogre fell upon him, and he looked up, that he saw Bradelf three feet in front of him. Bard swallowed hard, tried very hard not to lose control of any bodily functions, and found himself frozen to the spot.

"Hello," said Bradelf, "Do you like football?"

"Yes," was all Bard could manage to say, as being this close to Bradelf made thinking very difficult, and speech almost impossible.

"Can we have a game later?" asked Bradelf.
Again, after swallowing hard, Bard could only manage to say "Yes".

With that, Bradelf smiled, and headed off to see Mr Whackham and Miss Payne.

Bard could not believe he had been that close to Bradelf, that he had not disgraced himself, and that he had agreed to play football with him at playtime. As he regained the ability to move, and, still trembling, headed towards his classroom, a thousand thoughts flashed through his mind. Suppose Bradelf missed the ball and kicked him, sending him flying into the net, or worse still tackled him, breaking every bone in his body.

As it was, at playtime, nobody wanted to play football if Bradelf was in the team, and so the two boys sat side by side and talked about football instead. Small children watched from a distance, and teachers held their whistles in readiness, as Bard very shakily became Bradelf's first and only friend.

Bard told Bradelf of his dream to become an enter-printer and buy his own football club, and Bradelf asked if he could be the striker for the team. Although they were fast becoming friends, Bard thought it wise not to upset his new pal, and readily agreed that he should be Elfield United's striker when he was a little bit older and had, of course, had a trial with the club.

On the way home, Bard thought to himself that he'd had a pretty good day. He had survived a close encounter with Bradelf, made him a friend, and potentially secured his first signing for the club. Now that is pretty good going for an editor, budding enter-printer and chairman-to-be of Elfield United.

That evening, during supper, Bard told his parents about his meeting with Bradelf–leaving out the bit about bodily functions and trembling inside–and how they had become friends. As no one in their right mind was going to play football with them, he was not sure how their friendship would develop, but he said he really liked Bradelf, and called him a gentle-giant.

Obviously, he was not a giant, or an ogre or a troll, and the doctor had apparently said he did not have Thrummy-cap syndrome. However, he was not the sort of boy that children, and particularly small children, want to approach, let alone make friends with.

Bard stopped talking and placed a perhaps over-sized piece of chicken into his mouth. His mother smiled, cocked her head to one side, and stared very proudly at her enter-printer son. While he chewed the over-sized piece of chicken, she reminded him that he too had been naughty in the past but now was a son that any mother would be proud of.

While he continued to chew the over-sized piece of chicken, wishing he had cut it in half, his mother told him of the importance of not judging people by how they looked, but by how they are inside. Yes, Bradelf was big, and could be clumsy, but he did not have two heads, was not an ogre, and like every other boy in Elfland, needed at least one good friend.

As Bard finally got very close to the point when he could swallow the chicken, his father came up with a truly brilliant idea, as fathers so often do. If nobody at school wanted to play football when Bradelf was on the pitch, why not start your own football team? Bard's father even agreed to be the coach.

Bard could now see where he got his enter-printer skills from, and thought it a most amazing idea. He could put something in the next edition of the comic inviting children to a club trial, and his father could place an invitation in the local newspaper. Bard chewed, and thought to himself that life could not get any better.

That night in bed, a very happy boy thought about what his mother had said about needing friends. Did he have enough money to eventually get a manager like Sir Alex Fungusson, or players like Ryan Giggles? And more importantly, he thought about what he could do with The Bard Comic to help other children who, like himself and Bradelf, needed a little help, and most of all, good friends.

4 COMIC RELIEF

When you are the editor of a comic, a budding enter-printer, a centre forward for your own football club, and the future owner of Elfield United, life is busy, exciting and very rewarding. Bard had developed his business skills, and had now conned a small army of people into contributing to his comic every month. It had several fun pages, but also a healthy eating page, a page about learning difficulties, an exercise page, and even a page for guest articles.

The football team was now meeting twice a week for training and playing matches in the local league. Bard had even managed to find a sponsor to provide the all-important kit. His father, who had once played for the Elfland second team (until a knee injury ended his career), proved to be an excellent coach, and his mother did the laundry and provided apple juice for the team.

Bradelf seemed to have lost his clumsiness, and was now not only fast and an amazing dribbler, but was also the highest scoring player on the team. His reputation had not totally faded, however, and more timid opponents would often experience the urgent desire to tie their boot laces as he approached, while small ball boys would still run for cover as he neared the sidelines.

On Saturday the 31st of February, which is a very important day in the Elfland calendar and a training day for the club, a small boy approached Bard, poked him in the ribs and told him he wanted to not only play for the club, but be a forward. Now poking anybody in the ribs is not a good idea if you want them to think kindly of you, and is a very silly idea indeed if Bradelf is standing right behind you.

With his legs dangling in the air, and his arms somehow jammed up his sleeves, the small boy, totally unaware as to why he was being held so high shouted repeatedly, "Put me down you Oaf". Poking people in the ribs as a way of gain their attention is bad enough, but calling a giant an Oaf, when he already has you hanging in the air, is really not the smartest of things to say.

Still not really understanding why he was being treated in this way, as he'd only wanted to play football, hitting the ground from the height he had been lifted did make him think twice about calling a giant an Oaf. As Bradelf was considering what to do next to this very rude boy, Bard told him that another boy was having a trial that afternoon, and to get his kit on if he wanted to be considered.

The other boy in question was none other than Gudh Elf, a friend from Bard's kiting days, and by all accounts, a very good midfielder. Without further ado, Bard's father made up two teams from the first and second eleven, and started the trial. Gudh was indeed good, and not only kept an eye on the ball, but tackled cleanly. The other little boy did not fare so well, and, lacking everything but energy, fell foul of Bradelf.

A somewhat heavy tackle from Bradelf saw the little chap fly, somersault, and land heavily on his back, knocking the wind clear out of him. Bradelf, keen to get on with the game, picked him up, stood him back on his feet and said, "Sorry about that." He then kicked the ball directly at Gudh, which resulted in a very fine goal.

"What's your name?" said Bard's father to the small boy, who was now thinking twice about playing football at this level, particularly if they were allowed to use giants.

"Hob" squeaked the small boy, who was, as Bard's father had suspected, a goblin, and a goblin that had just had a near-death experience at the hands, or rather feet, of a giant.

Taking him by the hand, Bard's father led Hob slowly and carefully towards the touchline, and into the care of his wife, who gave him a glass of apple juice while checking that he still had two arms and two legs, and that they were in roughly the right places.

"I can't offer you a place in our first team, or the second team for that matter, but you are more than welcome to join the club," said Bard's father with his coach's hat on.

"Cheers mate," said Hob rather rudely as he hobbled off to get changed.

As he watched the small boy head off, Bard's father thought to himself about his early days in the game, the trials he had been offered, and the courage it takes to at least try.

As he passed Bradelf, who happened to be standing with his back to him, Hob could not help himself, and picked up a stick, which he threw in the direction of Bradelf's head. Fortunately for Bradelf, the stick missed him by a mile,

and very, very fortunately for Hob, Bradelf turned, looked him straight between the eyes, and smiled. Feeling rather silly, and extremely fortunate that every single bone was still inside his body, he sloped off home.

The following Saturday, Bard was pleased to see that Hob had turned up for football practice. Bard noticed that his father was quite strict with Hob, but praised him every time he did well. When they stopped for a break, Bard went over to Hob and started chatting. He asked him where he went to school, as he could not remember seeing him before, and was somewhat shocked when Hob said that he went to a special school.

Bard had always thought that Wizardton Primary School was very special, as the buildings and classrooms were very nice, and the playground and sports field were amazing. So Bard could not help himself, and asked Hob just what was so special about his school. He half expected him to boast about his school, and say how big the playing field was, but instead Hob lowered his head and spoke quietly.

Hob explained that it was a school for children that really, really struggled in school to learn to read and stuff, or who could not help themselves, and were naughty all the time. Bard asked why Hob was there, and Hob explained that it was because he could not sit still, he did silly things, and when the teachers tried to help him, he would kick them, or try to knock their glasses off.

Bard sat quietly listening to Hob and thought about his own past. He only stopped Hob when, perhaps getting a little carried away by the attention he was getting from Bard, Hob told of the time he had gotten into a fight with three trolls, an ogre and two green orcs. That one small goblin boy could survive such a fight would be remarkable, but to make them cry and run home to their mummies, was surely just beyond belief.

On the way home, Bard told his father about what Hob had said (though he left out the bit about making trolls cry) and the special school he attended. He wondered if the doctor that had helped him so much, and was looking after Bradelf, could also help Hob. It was time for some expert help, so they decided to ask Mrs Elf what could be done.

During supper, Bard told his mother about Hob and his problems, but steered clear of any mention of green orcs, as he did not want his mother to think that Hob told fibs and kicked teachers. Bard's mother listened to his every word. Once he had finished talking, she said it was a matter of time and place. This meant nothing to Bard, but his father nodded, knowing exactly what she meant.

Just like when Bradelf's mother had appeared at her side just at the moment when Bradelf was causing mayhem in the playground all those weeks ago, Bard's mother needed to be in the right place at the right time to talk to Hob's mother. This was not going to be easy, as, to date, neither of Hob's parents had been seen at football practice, and Bard's mother did not know where they lived.

Again, Bard's father came to the rescue, illustrating (for the second time, in a very short space of time) just where Bard's own enter-printer genius came from. Bard's father suggested inviting all the club member's parents to a raffle, which would be held in the sports hall in order to raise funds for the club. Of course, Hob's parents might not attend, but it had to be worth a try, and might raise some money for the club, if nothing else.

Invitations were handed out among the boys, the hall was booked, and the raffle prizes were collected. Now, all that was needed was for Hob's parents to turn up, and an amazing stroke of luck. Fortunately, Hob remembered to give the invitation to his mother. She was over the moon, and agreed with her husband Bob, to attend the raffle.

As it turned out, they did not need an amazing stroke of luck, as Fate stepped in and lent a hand. Not Fate as in good fortune, but Fate the sister of one of the boys, who, although a very nice young lady, did not suffer fools lightly.

Being a black belt in digiteridoo, (not the Australian musical instrument the didgeridoo, if you can call it that, but the martial art that uses just the fingers and toes), Fate had learnt how to perform several fearful blows. Having had a glass or three of fizzy pop, Hob got very angry, and when he bumped into Fate, attempted one of his infamous kicks.

His kick failed to reach the intended target, while the blows delivered by Fate were not only deadly accurate, but they did not conform to the Queensbury Rules, and left him on the floor squealing in pain, and seriously doubting if he would ever reach fatherhood. Every boy in the room had felt the power and pain of Fate's final kick, and one small boy fainted as a consequence.

While Bob Goblin comforted his son, and hoped Hob wouldn't be a soprano forever, Hob's mother started weeping out of a mixture of embarrassment and anger. It was at this point that Mrs Elf sidled up to Hob's mother, and offered her a nice cup of tea, and a shortbread biscuit. As Hob was taken outside in case he was sick (as often happens following a breach of the Queensbury Rules) the two ladies chatted.

They talked about diet and behaviour, fish oils and the growing brain. Mrs Elf promised to visit Hob's mother, Rob–short for Roberta–the next day, and bring a book all about what you can do to help children who struggle in school. Meanwhile, all the boys in the room were staying well clear of Fate, and adopting the pose of a football player in a defensive wall during a free kick, if she came anywhere near them.

It had been a bad day for Hob, and a lesser chap might have needed counselling from a tricky cyclist following such a beating by a girl. Even a troll having a very bad hair day could not have inflicted so much pain in such a short space of time. It had been so bad, that two boys had taken the next day off school with imaginary pains from just seeing the attack and hearing Hob's groans.

As it turned out, Fate had not dealt a fatal blow. In fact, she had done only what was required to ward off Hob's attack. However, in the tear-filled eyes of every boy in the room, he was dead meat, or at the very least, would never sing in a boy band other than a Bee Gees tribute group.

This strange twist of fate, or more likely, kick of Fate, was to be a turning point in Hob's troubled life. His mother kept in touch with Mrs Elf, helped out on training days at the club, and followed, to the letter, Mrs Elf's rules on keeping Hob's diet healthy, and giving him fish oils, vitamins and minerals every single day.

After just two months, Hob was less active and more able to concentrate. He didn't get angry without good reason, and no longer lashed out, or kicked people who annoyed him. He had, in fact, bumped into Fate one day-not literally but metasomethingly-and, despite feeling for a fleeting moment that he might faint, had managed to say "Hello" and apologise for trying to hit her.

As they chatted, Hob discovered that Fate was a very nice person (well for a girl that is). Fate explained how martial arts should only ever be used in self-defence, or the defence of others, and that you should not go around hitting people. Boys should certainly never, ever hit girls, Fate said, even if it is your annoying sister. Poor Hob had learnt this lesson the hard way, but it was certainly one he would never forget for the rest of his life.

Not only were things going much better at school, but on Tuesday the 25th of June, which of course is National Day in Slovenia, and still celebrated by some older elves out of respect for their foreign cousins, Hob received an official invitation from the football club to join the second team as a midfielder. There could not have been a happier boy anywhere in Elfland, or Slovenia for that matter, on that day.

The headmaster of the special school that Hob attended was just so impressed with the changes he had seen, that he asked Hob's mother to make an appointment with his secretary to come in and see him. The headmaster explained that he was particularly pleased with the changes in Hob's behaviour and his newly found ability to learn. He even suggested that Hob transfer to his local primary school at the beginning of the next term. The headmaster also wanted to find out more about what had caused these miraculous changes in young Hob, which caused Rob to wax lyrical - which means talk forever.

When, at last, Rob stopped talking, and Mr Swotham was finishing his third pot of tea, it was decided to invite Mrs Elf to visit the school, so that she could give him further information about helping children through diet and exercises. He also wanted to get the doctor, who had treated Bard and Bradelf, to visit the school, and give a talk to the parents.

The Good Doctor did come to the school, and not only did he talk to all the parents, he also gave a long talk to the staff about how the brain grows, and what can make it go wrong. Mr Swotham was so impressed, that after talking to the school Governors, in such a way that they thought it was their idea, he started using the doctor's ideas in school.

The school dinner became very healthy, all the snacks in the tuck shop were checked to make sure they did not contain bad things, and every day the children did special exercises. Some of the teachers went on special training days to have more lectures from the doctor, and the parents came in once a week to learn about diet and fish oils.

Things went so well, that after just two terms, all the children were really improving, and lots of them could be moved to their local schools. The school won an award; the Governors were very pleased with themselves, and Mr Swotham went on to receive an MBE. All these good things happened because, one small boy, on a boring day when it was pouring with rain, decided to make a comic.

5 THE GUDH, THE BARD AND THE UGLI

Gudh Elf and Badh Elf first met many moons ago while they were flying their kites in the park. Their friendship grew when Gudh had a trial with Bard United, and was selected to play for the club's prestigious first team. The Bard (as Badh Elf was now known by everyone) had also met the giant Bradelf - who wasn't really a giant - and the three of them were soon firm friends, and essential to the winning streak of Bard United.

Little Hob, a truly likeable character, had recently been selected to play in Bard United's second team. He and Bard would often have a kick around during the lunch break with Bradelf and few other boys in school.

Little Hob's football skills were improving by the day, and he no longer risked life and limb, even when tackling Bradelf. The giant Bradelf, who wasn't really a giant, could not help but smile, as the cheeky little chap deprived him of the ball and quickly passed it to Bard, who flicked it into the goal. At this rate,

Hob would soon be playing in the first team, and fulfilling a (fairly recent) lifetime dream.

Kick-about over, the boys sat on a low wall and talked about football, of course, while hoping the grass stains on their knees would fade before they got home, and rubbing mud into their trousers rather than waiting for it to dry out so they could brush it off later. It was at this point, that a boy tripped over Bradelf's outstretched legs, and spun round in an attempt to regain his balance. This caused his satchel to swing out and strike Hob full in the face. As Hob fell backwards, his legs shot up, tripping the unfortunate boy for the second time and causing him to fall and land on top of Bard.

As if this was not bad enough, as Hob fell backwards his right arm flew up, and the index finger of that hand ended up in Bradelf's left nostril. This, in turn, caused Bradelf to jerk suddenly to his right, which sent two small boys flying into a flowerbed.

Seeing so many boys flying in every direction caused Miss Payne, who was on playground duty, to blow her whistle, and start praying that they were not returning to the mayhem once caused by Bradelf. She need not have worried. As the dust cleared, Bradelf himself helped the others to their feet, dusted off the two small boys, and finally carried a sobbing girl to her.

The sobbing girl had been in the playground the day that Bradelf had caused mayhem, even though it was not May, and thinking that it was about to happen again, did what you do on occasions such as this, and had burst out crying. That Bradelf did not, in fact, eat her alive, and had picked her up very gently and taken her to "Miss", did little to comfort her, and she

continued - albeit totally unnecessarily - to sob for a further full twenty minutes. Still comforting the sobbing girl, Miss Payne blew her whistle again, and normality was restored to the playground.

The boy who had triggered the chain of events, which lead to Miss Payne blowing her whistle in sheer terror, was still trying to free himself from his satchel strap. During the kerfuffle, it had trapped his right arm. In the desperate struggle to free himself, he knocked over the two small boys that Bradelf had only just picked up, tripped over his own feet, and, with three of his limbs flailing, fell to the ground.

Yet again, it was the giant Bradelf, who wasn't really a giant, who came to the rescue, picking him up, and then releasing him from the satchel which was clearly possessed and intent on doing the poor young man some serious mischief. Now, as if that was not bad enough, once freed from the malevolent satchel, he did no more than stamp on it, partly out of anger, but also to signal its defeat.

Bad move. In doing so, he broke every pencil, crayon and pen that it contained, causing ink, and tiny pieces of crayon to cover all of his books and last night's homework. Unfortunately, he would only discover this later, when, in the classroom, he would put his hand into the offending satchel to take out a book, and would end up covering himself, and the girl sitting next to him, with black ink.

Bard had never seen anything quite like it, and suddenly realised what an accident waiting to happen really meant.

"What is your name?" asked Bard.

"Hob" replied the boy, who was attempting to put his right foot back into his shoe, while trying to lower his underpants, which were now at chest level, and tuck his shirt back into his trousers.

"Hob?" asked Bard.

"Yes, Hob Nob" replied the boy, as he attempted to reposition his tie, which caused his shirt to part company with his trousers again.

Now for those of you that do not know, and why should you, there are ordinary, everyday sort of goblins, and there are noble goblins who always go by the name of Nob. Looking at the boy, who was now trying to tuck his shirt into his trousers yet again, it was difficult, if not impossible, to imagine that Hob was a goblin of noble (posh) birth.

Later that day, during the short break, Bard spotted Hob Nob again. Well, you couldn't really miss him. Apart from the fact that his clothes were in total disarray and carrying mud and dust from the fall earlier, they were now covered in black ink too. And I do mean, covered. Bard walked towards him, not really knowing why, or indeed what he might say to the poor dishevelled boy.

As Bard approached, Hob looked up and said "Dyspraxia."

"What?" asked Bard, unsure if this was a very rude word used by posh goblins when really miffed.

"This," he said, "All this." Poor Hob looked as though he was going to cry, and Bard was about to comfort him with a manly hug when he remembered the ink that seemed to cover Hob's entire body and thought better of it.

At this point, Miss Payne approached the two boys, and Bard said "Dyspraxia," really hoping that it was not a very rude word used by posh goblins when they were really, really upset.
"Thank you, Bard," said Miss Payne with a smile, and, turning to Hob, who really did look like a chimney sweeps assistant, said "I think you had better come with me so I can clean you up a bit".

Bard had always felt kindly towards Miss Payne. Not just because he had conned her into writing pieces for his comic, but because she always cared for boys like Hob. However, on this occasion, he thought she was going to need a miracle unless she planned on placing Hob into a washing machine fully clothed. With that very silly thought in his mind, Bard wandered off, hoping that when he told his mother later about Hob, that she would not buy a huge washing machine with which to launder the entire football team after a match.

When Bard did tell his mother about the events of the day, she smiled, and cocked her head to one side as she listened. It was the sort of smile that showed she could see the funny side of the story, and who could not, but one that also showed of the sorrow she felt for the poor boy. When the story was finally over, Bard's mother said that perhaps she should have a word with Miss Payne in the morning.

Not only did she take the trouble to see Miss Payne the very next morning, but she took with her one of the books that had been written by the Good Doctor which had helped Bard all that time ago. Miss Payne said that she had no idea until the day before that Hob Nob was so dyspraxic, and that she would find the right time to talk to his parents.

As it happens, it was certainly not the right time for Hob. Unfortunately the events that were to follow later that day made it occur, but for all the wrong reasons. While he was getting dressed after gym, Hob bent over to put on his socks. This unfortunately caused his bare bottom to come into contact with a very hot water pipe. The pain caused Hob to stand up very quickly, which brought his head into contact with a hard wooden shelf. This, in turn caused his knees to buckle, which was when his chin struck the hard wooden bench.

Matron said it was a severe case of gun-cushion, and that she would need to keep a close eye on him. Matron also recommended that Hob's parents should be called immediately, if not sooner. When they arrived, they found poor Hob with a very red bottom, a plaster on his chin, and an egg on his head which was covered with a really silly looking rubber ice pack that matron had provided. He was a sorry sight.

As Mr Nob carried Hob to the car, his modesty almost protected by the small towelling gown that matron had provided, at least three children got a glimpse of his now very red bottom.

Miss Payne took the opportunity to say she hoped he would be OK and would pop round later after school. I am sure Hob's bottom, chin, and head would not agree, but Miss Payne thought this was the perfect opportunity to talk about dyspraxia.

As soon as the school day was over, Miss Payne collected various items of clothing that had been left in the changing room and put them in Hob's satchel. Oh dear. Having done so, she headed off to the car park, and from there to Noblis Hall to visit Hob. We can only hope that Mrs Nob has a very fine washing machine, rubber gloves, and some very good stain remover, which of course she will need when she opens the satchel.

Even small children will know, that if you have had a really bad bang to the head, you should lie quietly in a darkened room, and not attempt to move. Not so Hob, who not only got up, but attempted to dress. Now when you are not very good at getting dressed even on a really good day, it is probably a very bad idea to try when you have a severe case of gun-cushion. With his head still in a deep fog, Hob managed to get his socks on, but then, unable to find his pants, attempted to put on his trousers.

For fear of bringing back painful memories and making even grown men feel queasy, I won't go into any detail other than saying Hob had a *zip injury*. This brought tears to his eyes immediately, and after a tiny delay, a blood-curdling scream escaped from his lips. On hearing Hob's scream,

Hob's parents came running, while a little old lady down the road called the police! Seeing the poor boy's condition, his father fainted and his mother took immediate action.

Just as Mrs Nob was settling Hob back into bed, and placing a cushion under her husband's head, there was a knock at the door. It was Miss Payne calling to see how Hob was getting on, and you can imagine her distress when she heard of the events of the last few minutes. Not wishing to disturb Hob, Mrs Nob suggested that they took tea in the conservatory.

With Hob tucked up safely in bed, this was the perfect opportunity for Miss Payne to bring up the subject of his dyspraxia. As Ariel Payne talked to Mrs Nob about poor Hob, Mrs Nob began to sob, and Ariel passed her a paper hanky, which she always carried with her as part of the job. Mrs Nob's tears were tears of happiness: at last someone had shown that they cared, understood the problem her son was facing, and knew what to do about it!

It would mean another family from Wizardton making the long journey to see the Good Doctor, but at least now there was hope, and Sid Sidebottom the chauffeur (when he was not being the gardener or handyman) would drive them there and back. So the call was made, and an appointment booked, which was hoped would see an end to poor Hob's constant accidents.

On the day of the appointment, the Good Doctor asked Mrs Nob lots and lots of questions, before asking Hob lots of questions too. Then the Good Doctor carried out lots and lots of tests on Hob. Fortunately, none of the tests hurt, and throughout the whole visit the Good Doctor teased Hob and made him laugh. The Good Doctor explained exactly what the problem was, and how some places, mainly in the back of Hob's brain, weren't working too well. The doctor even suggested that they should stop on the way home for an ice cream.

The next day in school, when Hob told Bard about what the Good Doctor had said, and what he now had to do, Bard said, "I knew it. It's your cherrybellbum". Hob had a list of exercises to do each day to help the back of his brain to work better, and so he hurried off to find Miss Payne, who had agreed to help him with them during the lunch break.

As the weeks passed, Hob mastered every one of his exercises, and when he returned to the clinic to see the Good Doctor, all the tests showed that indeed the back of his brain was working much better. Hob still had to do other exercises each day, but he got to play a really cool computer game each day at home, and it was clear to everyone that he was improving.

One day, as Hob sat next to Bard having lunch, Bard asked Hob if he would do something for him. Hob agreed readily, and Bard did what he did best, deli-plating that is, and asked Hob to write him a story about what it is like to have dyspraxia, and how it makes you feel inside.

"It makes you feel bad," said Hob "Silly, stupid and rubbish. I hated it when the other children laughed at me".

Hob wrote his story, which was not only very interesting, but also funny, and sad in places. He explained how hard his life had been, constantly having accidents, and struggling to get his fingers to do the simplest of tasks. Hob made the story light-hearted, and even told the tale about tripping over Bradelf's feet, and the chain reaction that followed. He also spoke of the many nights he had cried himself to sleep after other children had laughed at his clumsiness.

Bard included the story in the next edition of The Bard Comic, and both Bard's mother and Miss Payne had to try very hard not to cry when they read of Hob's secret suffering. Many children came forward and said that they too had felt they were rubbish because they were struggling to read, or could not write nicely, and this had made them very sad.

One lunch time, as Bard, Bradelf, Hob and Hob were having lunch, Bard said to Hob Nob, "What is that?" pointing to a strange orange fruit in his lunch box.

"It's an ugli fruit," said Hob.

With that, Bard said, "That is going to have to be your nickname from now on."

So it was, that Hob became Ugli, and the Gudh, the Bard and the Ugli came about.

Weeks became months, and Ugli, as he was now affectionately known by all, including the Good Doctor, made amazing progress, not just with his balance and not having accidents every five minutes, but with his handwriting and reading too. This was due, according to Bard, to the fact his eyes were working better after the computer game helped fix his cherrybellbum.

As Editor-in-Chief of The Bard Comic, as he now called himself, even though he was the only editor, Bard had to read everything that was to go into the comic, and the pieces Miss Payne wrote every month had taught him a lot about how the brain can glitch, and how it could be fixed. Bard now knew all the names of all the things that could make learning difficult and would use his comic to tell as many children as possible about them.

For a young elf he wasn't doing too badly. He already was the Editor-in-Chief of a very important comic, the sort-of Chairman of a football club, an enter-printer, and a first rate deli-plater. Could life get any better? Well it could, and it did. By helping so many other people, Bard's life grew richer and happier with every passing day.

6 HUMPHREY

Mr and Mrs Boggart lived in what had always been a quiet, respectable part of Wizardton. Now, for those of you who aren't particularly familiar with the "little people", as they are sometimes known, a Boggart is created when an elf and a fairy get married and have a baby. This happened to be exactly what Mr and Mrs Boggart did, and the result was a beautiful little boy called Humphrey.

Now I say a beautiful little boy, and that he was and indeed still is, but oh dear, looks can be so deceiving. Bogey, as his friends (which were mainly goblins) called him, was usually up before the birds, and did not stop to rest until the crows were snoring. I mention the goblins, not because I personally have anything against them, but because they are (and no one can deny it) very cheeky by nature.

At 3.57am on Tuesday the 18th of June, Mrs Boggart was not only fast asleep in the marital bed, but dreaming of fame and fortune. Both she and her husband were keen members of Wizardton Amateur Dramatic Society, and although she knew in her heart she would never make it to Folly Wood and the silver screen, a girl can dream. But not for long, as at precisely

4.03am Humphrey was up, and from then on no one could sleep.

Many moons ago, when Humphrey was still a baby Boggart, he had learnt how to climb out of his cot. Following this discovery, Mr and Mrs Boggart had decided to take it in turns to occupy Humphrey. This way, at least one of them could remain horizontal. With Humphrey fully awake, sleep was not an option. When it fell to Mrs Boggart to keep Humphrey occupied, Mr Boggart liked to study genealogy.

Now, for those of you who might not know, genealogy has nothing to do with rubbing old lamps, or indeed coming out in lumps or bumps as a consequence, as that would be genie-allergy, but involves looking up ones family history. So, as Humphrey ran riot in the house, and Mrs Boggart attempted, without success, to keep him quiet, Mr Boggart delved into his family background.

Actually, and I only mention this in passing, Mr Boggart had traced his family origins back to the West Riding of Yorkshire, and his good lady wife's family tree back to Lancashire, both in the North of England, which of course was nowhere near where they were living now. You may be surprised to hear this, or indeed doubt my words as being fanciful, but it is no more than the truth.

Boggarts were plentiful in both the counties of Yorkshire and Lancashire, and only migrated to Elfland during the War of the Roses, which had nothing to do with Flower Power (that happened much later on in history). That this is true is borne out by various expressions still used to this day in the old Boggart dialect. From time to time, even Mr Boggart would say, "Tis real is that." Meaning he found something especially interesting.

While Mr Boggart sat in bed wondering why there was not a South Riding, Mrs Boggart struggled to control Humphrey *and* cook breakfast. Young Humphrey was a force to be reckoned with, and Mrs Boggart looked forward to that moment in time when he would pass through the school gate and some normality would return, if only for a few hours.

While Mrs Boggart looked forward to being able to clean, shop and cook in peace, Humphrey's teacher, Ms Stake, was bracing herself for yet another day in the classroom. Ms Stake had hoped that having a new classroom assistant in the form of Trixie Pixie, a spritecology graduate no less, might help control Humphrey, but no. Now she had Humphrey hurtling around the classroom with Trixie in tow, while a particularly rude group of goblins chanted, "Go Bogey, go".

The summer holidays were rapidly approaching, and Ms Stake could not wait to get away for her long awaited trip to Trolland. In fact, the more she thought about it, the more she thought about seeking employment there and never returning. She had now awoken in the middle of the night, which is rarely, if ever, actually in the middle of the night, and found herself screaming, "BOGEY!" Clearly, something had to be done.

After a particularly stressful day, during which Humphrey had wound up four goblins and two elves to such a point that two other teachers and the school nurse had to be called in to restore order, Ms Stake was at breaking point. After school, and in Mrs Sidebottom's (pronounced Siddy-Botham) office, Ms Stake said something she had never thought she would ever say to the principle; namely, "It's him or me".

The headmistress said that she was sure it was just a matter of being over tired at the end of a long term and that all Ms Stake needed was a nice, long holiday, after which everything would be fine.
"I repeat," said Ms Stake, "It is him or me. One of us has to go". Oh dear. Things had clearly reached breaking point and something had to be done.

Mr and Mrs Boggart were summoned to Mrs Sidebottom's office, and were told, in no uncertain terms that unless things changed very much for the better, Humphrey would not be welcome at the school next term. Mrs Sidebottom said arrangements would be made, and a letter would be put in the post concerning Humphrey's future education. Not good.

After the meeting Hardley, Mrs Boggart's husband, took Humphrey to the park to let off steam, and Mrs Boggart sat in the garden and sobbed. What had gone wrong? How could this be happening to them? What could be wrong with the boy? Slowly, she started having doubts, and blaming herself. Was it something that she had done during her pregnancy? Surely the two wine gums she had eaten on her birthday when she was eight months pregnant could not have caused all this.

Suddenly, she got up and rushed indoors. Trembling, and not altogether sure she knew what she was doing, Mrs Boggart called a teacher she had met at a weekend cookery school. This was not the first time Avery Longbottom had received a call such as this, and he listened patiently as Mrs Boggart explained about Humphrey.

As it was, Avery was the very man she needed. Not only had he been the one to advise Mr Elf all those months ago, but he had, by chance, just read a blog saying that the Good Doctor who had helped Bard so much was now doing consultations over Skype. Avery gave Mrs Boggart the Good Doctor's telephone number and told her to stop worrying, as he was sure everything would be fine.

As soon as her husband returned from the park with Humphrey, Mrs Boggart told him everything that Avery had told her. Hardley was on the internet in seconds, and before you could say a word, he had sent the Good Doctor an email asking for help. While Mrs Boggart fed, bathed, and attempted to get Humphrey in bed, Hardley read every page of the Good Doctor's website.

Imagine the joy in the household when, in the morning, they discovered a reply to their email, and the possibility of a consultation via Skype for that very afternoon, if they were available. While Hardley emailed the Good Doctor, accepting the appointment, his wife, Honeybee, wondered if she needed to do her hair, and put on her best dress in readiness for the consultation.

As it was, occupying Humphrey for the morning took up all of the couple's time and effort, and before they knew it, Mr and Mrs Boggart were sat in front of the computer and chatting to the Good Doctor. The doctor needed a great deal of information about, not only Humphrey, but also the Boggart family history. Would you believe, the Good Doctor actually laughed when Hardley told him of his research, and his Yorkshire roots?

In between chatting to Hardley and Honeybee, the Good Doctor asked

Humphrey lots of questions, and kept him laughing throughout the hour and a half they were online. When Humphrey told the Good Doctor what the goblins called him, the doctor laughed, as few can resist goblin humour, but then he suggested that "Boogie" might suit Humphrey better.

By the end of the session, Honeybee and Hardley knew exactly what the problem was, and perhaps more importantly, what they could do to fix it. Boogie, in common with many young Boggarts and Goblins, apparently had a sugar addiction. Imagine, still in short trousers and an addict already! The Good Doctor explained that some children cannot handle simple sugars all that well. They become addicted to them, and the rest, as they say, is history.

Boogie's parents had to put Boogie on a strict diet, monitoring everything he ate and drank. Boogie also had to take omega 3-6 supplements, vitamins and minerals, and as the Good Doctor had said, would have to go "cold turkey" for two weeks. Since Boogie quite liked cold meats, he was not really too upset at the thought of this. However, not being allowed to have sweets and puddings and fizzy cola, was just too much to bear.

The Good Doctor had told the family that the first two weeks of the new diet would be hell, and he was not wrong. As Boogie reacted to the dramatic reduction in simple sugars, he was not only extremely active, but very, very angry. Honeybee and Hardley were up most nights–as probably were half of Wizardton–as Boogie ranted and raved day and night. Was this ever going to be worth the effort?

On Tuesday the 9th of July, Mr and Mrs Boggart overslept. For years they had never needed to set the alarm, as Humphrey would be climbing all over them, or crashing about the house long before the day was anywhere near dawning. In a panic, they threw themselves out of bed and ran into Boogie's bedroom, fearing the worst. In fact, Boogie was fast asleep, breathing gently, and would you believe it, looking almost angelic.

For the first time in what seemed like living memory, Honeybee and Hardley sat quietly in the conservatory, and sipped their morning coffee. Hardley had taken a few days off work to be on hand during the "cold turkey" phase of the treatment, and now wondered if it would be possible to return to work before all his holidays were used up. Today, at least, he decided he would stay at home, as he was not convinced as yet, that this was really happening.

But it was. As Honeybee and Hardley enjoyed their second cup of coffee, Humphrey appeared at the door, and asked very politely what was for breakfast. He played quietly while the Full Elfish was prepared, and asked again politely if they could have a day out at the adventure park near Fairy Down Meadow. Still not convinced that this was really happening, Boogie's parents readily agreed, and prepared to set off.

It was while they were at the park that it happened. They were not sure at first if it was down to the excitement of the day, or a result of the hearty breakfast, but when it continued well into the late afternoon, Mrs Boggart, in particular, was to say the least, somewhat concerned. The "It" in question, and I am going to have to be careful so as not to offend the more delicate reader, was what Mrs Boggart feared might be terminal wind.

Once home, Mrs Boggart tried calling the Good Doctor, while her husband opened all the windows and doors and asked Humphrey whether he would like to go outside and play in the garden. Having left a message on the doctor's answerphone, Mrs Boggart used up an entire aerosol of her favourite Fairy Fragrance air spray, and sent her husband to fetch another half a dozen cans from the corner shop.

It was while Mr Boggart and Humphrey were at the shop that the Good

Doctor called back. Mrs Boggart found the conversation very difficult, but, eventually managed to bring herself to tell the Good Doctor of her real concerns that, Boogie, as he called her son, might have an advanced form of terminal wind. Before regaining his usual professional dignity, the Good Doctor erupted into near hysterical laughter.

He explained that wind was very common following a change in diet, especially after the introduction of so much fruit and, in particular, green vegetables. He mentioned that it was not at all unusual, and was a common side effect, notably in children of Elf or Goblin extraction. In fact, many goblin boys between the ages of four and six tend to bottom-burp as a result of any dietary change, he explained.

Mrs Boggart was relieved to hear this, but could have really done without the indelicate medical explanation that followed. Apparently, between the inside of every boy and his underpants, there is only the snippet valve. Following a little "digestive wobble" (as the Good Doctor put it), the valve can fail. By mentioning that his own research had indeed found the genetic link to Elves and Goblins, the Good Doctor attempted to reassure Honeybee still further. This, of course, was quite unnecessary.

Mrs Boggart, who was of a delicate constitution, had heard enough, but the Good Doctor was on a roll. With great authority, he informed her, that the Far Trolls of Northern Trolland never gain control of their snippet valves, which is why they are now found only in isolated communities deep within the fir tree forests of Far Trolland.

When Mrs Boggart put the phone down, she was quite flustered. However, she was totally reassured that in a matter of a few days the situation would be resolved. Fortunately, it was summer, and so the windows and doors could be kept open day and night, and the now totally compliant Humphrey could be persuaded to play outside all day.

Naturally, the Good Doctor was, of course, right, and everything returned to normal within two weeks, which was lucky, as the corner shop had run out of air freshener. Mr Boggart had been able to return to work before all his holiday days were used up. But Mrs Boggart still had to tackle the tricky business of getting Humphrey back into his old school.

What Mrs Boggart did not know, was that if Humphrey was allowed back into school, his new form teacher would be Ariel Payne. Ms Stake had met someone during her holiday in Trolland. Unlike many holiday romances, it looked like it was set to last. Bee Stake had in fact become engaged to Mr Elphin Tiddly, had handed in her notice, and planned to return to Northern Trolland, where the pair were dreaming of purchasing a tavern in the woods and living happily ever after.

Clearly, Ms Stake knew nothing of the Good Doctor's research into the habits of the Far Trolls of Northern Trolland. Alternatively, perhaps Ms Stake, who had suffered severe sinusitis for most of her life, would find fifty drunken Far Trolls packed into her tavern more acceptable than one small boy winding up a group of mischievous goblins.

Boogie Boggart was allowed to return to school, and did indeed find himself in Ariel Payne's class. This was a blessing in disguise, as not only did she have a bit of a soft spot for him, but with her special training, she was able to help Boogie to catch up on all of his school work. He did his best to work hard in class, avoided goblins, and even did all his homework on his own, and without having to be nagged.

When the whole family next spoke with the Good Doctor, he was overjoyed at Boogie's progress, and said that he was so pleased that he was in Ariel Payne's class and doing so well. He said that he didn't think they would need to chat again and wished the Boggarts well in life. The Good Doctor, Mr and Mrs Boggart, and Boogie Boggart were all very happy, and who wouldn't be?

7 GIRL POWER

If you have been reading these little stories about Wizardton and Elfton, you may have been thinking, and I would say quite rightly, that there has been little mention of girls. Well, the thing is, in Elfland, there are more boys than girls with learning problems and silliness syndrome. (This is probably true about where you live too). Also, and this is a fact, in Elfland most girls have fairy magic in their hearts and therefore tend to be goody two-shoes.

Now, I am not saying that *all* the girls in Elfland were perfect. (Even in a fairy story, no one would believe that!). However, with the exception of Lollilou and Freya Winterbottom, who shared a habit of wiggling their noses and then giggling, most were very well behaved. Having said that, at one time in Spritely Minster, there were many rumours of a scary gang of girls.

The so-called gang in question was, in truth, just a group of girls that had got a bit carried away. Having heard about girl power on the news, the girl gang had given themselves really silly nicknames. Each and every one of them was a fairy by birth, and as you can imagine nobody's blood was going to turn to ice when faced by Scary Hairy Mary Fairy, who didn't even have a beard.

Be that as it may, Hairy Mary, Sweaty Betty and Smelly Ellie, formed a girl gang, and then did what members of a feisty fairy gang do best: they sat around talking about it. Even so, word soon got around, and before long Silly Lily and Smiley Kylie had joined the gang as well.

It was not just other girls who heard about the gang and really rated them, but also a good number of boys as well. More timid boys took to crossing to the other side of the street if the gang were spotted, and one poor chap seeing the gang in full flight, (actually just stood by a bus stop) wet himself. Oh dear.

Silly Lily had given herself the nickname because she could not read very well. Silly Lily felt she was stupid (and it rhymed, of course). One day, after school, when the gang met up to sit around and talk about what a great girl gang they were, Sweaty Betty (who incidentally was not particularly sweaty, apart from her feet perhaps, and only then in summer) asked Silly Lily if she was OK? Lily started crying.

Hairy and Sweaty sat beside her, and giving her a girl power hug asked her what the matter was. During the last lesson of the day, Silly Lily's teacher, Miss Fortune, had asked each child in the class to stand up and read a paragraph aloud. Lily had really struggled, which made her feel totally bad, but then, as she was crossing the playground, a boy from Lily's class had told her that she must be really stupid if she could not read, and this had upset her even more.

While Sweaty comforted Lily, insisting that she was not stupid, Hairy planned on how they would teach the young man not to mess with a girl gang, and just what girl power was all about. Hairy asked for the boy's name, and on hearing it, she beamed. Eddie Ramsbottom was well known in the area for not being a very nice boy, and it was rumoured that his maternal grandfather was a Bogle, and there's not much worse than that.

Hairy declared a meeting of the Action Committee, and a most terrible plan of action was put into place. Smelly knew for a fact that pretty well all the goblins that lived on the south side of Spritely Minster, had the habit of meeting at the brook near Sandy Bottom to skinny-dip of an early evening. All they had to do now was to get down to the brook unnoticed, and await their chance.

The plan was simple. It involved no more than waiting until Eddie Ramsbottom was in the brook with his friends. Once Eddie was swimming in the brook, the girls would carefully remove his clothes from the water's edge. They would only return Eddie's clothes to the water's edge after he'd been forced to walk home naked as the day he was born. Sweaty volunteered to do the dastardly deed. Since Sweaty had older brothers, she was unlikely to be flustered should one of the boys leave the brook before the deed was done.

Sweaty hid in the tall grass awaiting her chance. In a flash, she had grabbed Eddies clothes and retreated to her hiding place. One by one, the boys left the brook, and eventually, Eddie, having searched every square inch of the bank, did the only thing he could, and started crying. Covering himself as best as he could, he headed for home. Unfortunately for him, part two of the cunning plan was now falling into place, and at every corner stood at least two girls.

An hour later, Eddie had finally reached the village green which he would have to cross to reach home. There was nowhere to hide. As he started the final sprint for home, two things happened. One, the local policeman spotted Eddie, causing him to wobble and nearly fall off his bike, before setting off after him in hot pursuit. Two, a small dog decided to join in the fun, and chased after Eddie's bottom.

With the little dog now in full flight, and closing in on Eddie's bare Ramsbottom, the police officer saw no need to hurry. He hummed quietly to himself and steered the bike vaguely in the direction of the fleeing boy. Eddie was screaming like a demented banshee. Certain that the fangs of the vicious beast would sink into his bottom at any second, Eddie threw himself over the garden hedge and into his garden.

As Eddie soon discovered, attempting to clear a three-foot holly hedge when you are not much taller than three feet yourself, and, need I remind you, naked as the day you were born, is not a very wise decision. Fortunately for Eddie, the vicious dog was no more than a Labradoddle puppy who really only wanted to play, as well the police constable knew. Eddie's screams of sheer terror had caused his mother to run out of the house, convinced that hoards of villainous ogres were attacking the village.

Instead, all she found was her young son, covered in mud and without a stitch of clothing, half hanging out of the holly hedge, and a police constable removing his notepad and pencil from his pocket, while a small dog tugged at his trouser legs. What she did not see was probably the most feared girl gang in Spritely Minster, if not the whole of Elfland, lurking in the bushes and chanting, "Girl power".

Needless to say, the police constable did not arrest the young boy, and after giving him a good ticking-off, mounted his bicycle and humming quietly to himself, rode off back to the police station. Eddie's mother and father did not, however, remain as calm as the constable, as they clearly wanted to know why their young son was running naked through the village.

Once everybody had calmed down, it was decided that the whole thing was just a prank. Only the coolest girl gang ever would know the real truth. However, it also meant that Eddie would become the butt, so to speak, of every schoolchild's jokes for days and weeks to come.

In school, Miss Fortune was growing ever more concerned about Lily Pari's struggle to read. As luck would have it, later that morning, Ariel Payne sat next to Miss Fortune in the Staff Room, and started telling her about how she was having certain children in the school tested in order to see whether their struggle to read was actually an eye tracking problem. Miss Fortune mentioned Lily, and asked Ariel if she might add her to her list of children.

Ariel, who was clearly very excited about the Good Doctor, as she called him, visiting the school, went on to explain what it was all about. Apparently, lots of young children can't make their eyes move in towards their nose. Of course, you have to do this when reading, otherwise you can't make them move across the page and read nicely.

Miss Fortune was really excited about what she had learnt, and she asked Lily to stay behind at the end of the morning, since she wanted to talk to her. When she did, she sat her down, and got her to look at the end of a pencil as she moved it towards her nose and back again. She explained that she was no expert, which is pretty obvious, but thought that her left eye was not moving in towards her nose as it should do.

Later that day, Lily told the other members of the girl gang about her eye, and Hairy Mary said she thought it would be brilliant if it could help her to read, but of course she would have to change her girl gang name. "Just imagine," said Sweaty, "Lil the Brill," and they all laughed. But it wasn't only the girls that were pleased; Lily's mother was too as she had been so worried about Lily's reading.

Well, the day finally came, and eventually the Good Doctor, as he was known, tested Lily's eye movements using his computer and some really neat 3D glasses. Not only did the left eye struggle to come in towards the

nose, but when she was reading, it seemed to have a mind of its own, and spent half the time going right to left. The Good Doctor asked Lily if she ever wrote letters and numbers back to front, and when she nodded, he said that he was amazed she could read at all.

The Good Doctor loaded some computer games onto Miss Payne's computer, gave Lily some 3D glasses, and then showed her how to play the games. They were fun games that involved splatting ogres and shooting at targets, but they would also get everybody's eyes doing what they should be doing, and before long, all the children reading.

Ariel Payne was beside herself with excitement. She soon had all the children playing the games in school each day. She also showed all the teachers what to look for if a child was struggling with their reading. She even arranged for the parents of all the children that were using the games, to come into school for a special evening. The children's parents were all thrilled with the progress they were making and Ariel Payne was able to give a special talk about healthy eating.

Just three months later, the Good Doctor returned to the school to retest all the children. Miss Fortune was given the job of testing the children's reading ages before he arrived. The results of the reading age tests would allow the Good Doctor to see if any improvement in the eye movements matched an improvement in their reading. When all the tests were completed, the Good Doctor, Miss Fortune and Ariel Payne, not to mention the children, were overjoyed at the results.

Each and every child had improved, but young Lily Pari had made the greatest progress. Not only were her computer scores brilliant, but her reading age had jumped up so much, that doubting the results, Miss Fortune asked Miss Payne to retest her. There was no doubt about it, her reading age had shot up, and with that, so did her confidence. From now on, no more "Silly Lily".

That evening, when the hottest girl gang in all of Elfland met on the village green, and the members all talked excitedly about Lil the Brill's test results, a second plan was launched. Plan B, as it would be known, would involve Lily writing a short story, and then somehow getting Miss Payne to let her read it out loud in front of the entire school. Innocent enough, you might think, but remember Plan B had been thought up by a really hip girl gang, and was therefore awesome.

The short story was all about the girl gang's first, and actually only, activity involving the very rude Eddie Ramsbottom. Of course, the names would be changed to protect the innocent. This was, as they say, a double edged sword, and the only innocent people to remain unscathed would be the members of the most famous girl gang ever.

Every child in Elfton knew about Eddie running naked through the streets, so when Lily read her short story in front of the whole school, which included all the teachers, she knew every eye would be looking at him. The story spoke of how bad not being able to read had made her feel, and how, one day, a very cruel boy had been very nasty to her, and had made her very sad.

As her story unfolded, the boy in question was named for the first time, causing girls to giggle uncontrollably, the boys to guffaw, the teachers to snigger, and the headmistress to start laughing out loud. From then on, any mention of the plight of "Little Willy" caused uproar in the assembly, and Eddie to die a thousand deaths.

In the staff room later that morning, Lily's story was on everyone's lips, and the childish humour that we should never lose, caused numerous grownup teachers to giggle at every mention of Little Willy. It was during this revelry over coffee, that Mrs Sidebottom herself first called the gang the "Sprite Girls," - a name that would remain with them forever.

Meanwhile in the playground, a queue of girls and two small boys waited impatiently to get the autographs of the coolest girl gang ever, and a group of goblins took turns at creeping up behind Eddie and barking, or calling out, "Has anyone seen Little Willy?" In tears, Eddie stood with his head lowered, and would have run away were it not for a kindly girl taking him by the hand and leading him off to Miss Payne.

The caring young lady was none other than Lily Pari, who, seeing Eddie burst into tears, felt compassion in her heart, and knowing that he now knew how she had once felt, decided he had suffered enough. The fairy magic in her heart would not only take away Eddie's pain, but would help him realise how heartless he had been in the past. As Miss Payne told him, "Eddie, what goes around, comes around".

Never again would any boy, and in particular goblin, mess with a Sprite girl, and Eddie would carry in his heart kindness and understanding forever. Childhood should be a time for fun, excitement and discovery, but sometimes things can go wrong and make you sad. When you are having a hard time, the last thing you need is another child making you feel worse. This was the lesson Eddie learnt the hard way.

No child should be bullied or teased for any reason whatsoever, so if you know of a child that is upset, even if you are not a fairy, see if you can find the magic in your heart, and offer your friendship. Together, you can tell a teacher or parent and, with the added strength of friendship, put an end to it.

A bully is a strange creature. It does not matter if a bully is an elf, a goblin, or even a troll, there is something that you need to know. They probably have problems of their own; they are almost certainly a coward, and if they were given a taste of their own medicine, they would most likely run home to their mummy crying like a baby. If you are being bullied, tell someone today, and if you have ever been a bully, just remember what happened to Eddie, and never do it again.

8 A TIC-CURLY SUBJECT

Tom Tickler, a young elf, was the sort of a son that any mother would be so proud of. He was tall and slim, with boyish good looks, and a mane of thick, blond hair. Indeed, he was a picture of elf. He was not only good in the classroom, but was a first-rate sportsman, and had the makings of a gentleman elf of some standing.

Tom lived with his parents and younger brother in an old farmhouse on the outskirts of Gnomemansland, surrounded by open fields that seemed to stretch out forever. They had orchards, a vegetable garden, a flower garden, formal flowerbeds, and meadows of sweet grass. All this was maintained beautifully by just one man and a boy.

Flikker Urist, the Scottish gardener, not only ensured that everything always looked perfect (even though this sometimes required him to wag a twisted finger at Ben Doone, his young helper) but he also cultivated the very finest fresh fruit, vegetables, and sweet smelling flowers. Regardless of the season, old Flik, as he was affectionately known, always managed to bring something to the kitchen door.

Of a summer's evening, once the boys had been sent upstairs to get ready for bed, Ellie Tickler liked nothing better than to sit quietly on the old flagstone patio and, sipping from a glass of Elderflower wine, stare at the far horizon, and dream. Intoxicated by the fragrance of jasmine and sweet azalea (not to mention the second glass of wine) Ellie often wondered if life could get any sweeter.

Dwight Tickler had made his name, and some would say his fortune, playing marbles at a national, and then international, level. When he had retired from the sport, he had invested his money wisely, and now occupied his time with his import/export business based in Switzerland, where a group of hard working gnomes ensured he paid little, if any, tax.

Mary Faerie, who had come to work on the farm when her mother, Fata, considered retirement, was the first to realise something was afoot when she heard Mr Tickler shouting very angrily down the phone. When the very official letters started arriving in the post, Mary grew even more concerned, and then of course, *it* happened.

There was a phone call, followed by shouting, and then the crash of something breaking. Dwight had always been a man who coped well under pressure (as a world-class marbles player, Dwight had gotten used to stress) but now the pressures of running his businesses during the recession were getting at him. Day by day, he became more and more angry, was not sleeping, and spent most of his time shouting at people down the phone.

Dwight's import business catered to the large number of expats, mainly from Scotland and Ireland, who now lived in Elfland. Each week, containers of Marmite, baked beans, bacon, black pudding, pork pies, sausages and custard powder arrived at the docks. A fleet of specially designed refrigerated lorries then distributed the goods across Elfland. However, as fuel prices rose, profits dwindled.

As fewer and fewer people wanted to purchase good luck charms, fairy

wishes, spells or fancy dress items, Dwight's export business suffered further. Interflora had cornered the market for lucky heather and children had lost interest in gentle fairies, preferring action-computer games involving ogres. It had even been suggested that some children doubted whether the Tooth Fairy really existed. Times were hard.

It was Tiny Tim, Tom's little brother, who first noticed a difference in Tom. At first, it was no more than blinking a lot when Tom was tired or stressed. Gradually the blinking worsened, happened a lot more and then Tom started curling his bottom lip. At first, the boy's father would get cross at Tom, and tell him to stop, but how do you stop doing something when it is not really you who is doing it?

On one particular day, while Dwight was having a really hard time dealing with a shipment of frozen haggis, Tom was feeling the stress in the household and was ticking badly. Tom's father lost the plot, and really shouted at Tom. His mother stepped between them, and told Dwight to leave Tom alone. "He needs help, not you shouting at him," said Ellie and steered Tom towards the kitchen.

Flikker, who was delivering fresh duck eggs to the kitchen, had heard the commotion and gave Ellie a knowing nod. Old Flik was so ancient that he knew almost everything, and in his broad Scottish accent he explained, "It'll be all the uproar in the hoose and too many sweeties or I'm a goats bottom!" With that, and a knowing smile, he shuffled off about his business.

Ellie sat her son down and looked him straight in the eye. Holding his gaze, she asked him if he had been eating sweets. He tried to look away, but a gentle hand guided him back, and he was forced to answer his mother's question. As the level of stress in the house had risen, he had started eating sweets, and when the tics started, he'd become more stressed, and so had eaten even more sweets.

Now everything was becoming clear to Ellie, but what to do about it? Somehow, she had to calm her husband, but she also had to find a way to stop Tom ticking and to stop Tim from wetting the bed, which he had started doing around about the same time as Tom had started ticking. Clearly Ellie needed to have a long, private talk with her husband, and then do some research on the internet.

It was while she was trawling the internet that Ellie found a book all about children with tics and other problems. She downloaded it immediately, and had read it cover to cover by the following morning. She had also emailed the author asking for help, and had a long talk with Dwight about how him being so stressed out was upsetting the boys so much.

The following morning, Ellie was exhausted, but at least now she understood why the boys were reacting in the ways they were. The Good Doctor she had emailed had replied and suggested that they have a chat over the phone.

Ellie felt in control again. She sat in her favourite spot in the garden and sipped her morning coffee, as old Flik pottered about in the long flower border.

Ellie's chat with the Good Doctor went very well, and it was decided that they would hold a family chat using Skype. Although the Good Doctor needed to focus on Tom, it was the ideal opportunity for him to help Tim as well, and to guide Dwight in the right direction. All Ellie had to do now was to get her "three young men", as she called them, in the right frame of mind for the family chat.

In fact, it could not have gone better! The Good Doctor had Tim laughing right from the start, slowly built up Tom's confidence, and gently nudged Dwight in the right direction. By the time the long chat was over, the boys were full of fun again, and Mr and Mrs Tickler were kissing and cuddling, and being thoroughly embarrassing (as parents often are).

Over the coming weeks, Dwight made major changes to his export business, and following a renewed interest in marbles, notably in the UK and USA, launched Dwight's Magic Marbles. Also, with a drop in fuel costs in Elfland put in place by the government to boost business, Dwight was able to expand his range of products to include chunky marmalade, tinned pilchards, fresh tripe and oven-ready Yorkshire puddings.

Within three weeks, Tim had stopped wetting the bed, and had gone back to being his usual happy-go-lucky self. With all the stress in the household gone, the worry centre in Tim's brain had also settled down, and the "to-pee or not-to-pee" centre, which lies just behind it, was back in control day and night. It also became apparent that he had his father's natural skill when it came to playing marbles, and would soon become the regional junior champion.

Tom's tics were beginning to settle down, and were now no more than a lot of blinking when he was tired, or if anyone mentioned tics in front of him, drawing attention to it. His mother, who was in regular contact with the Good Doctor, had arranged an appointment for him to visit the clinic, as it was felt that it would be wise to carry out some tests, and then maybe add some other treatments.

As the clinic was a long way away, Ellie decided that they would make a fun weekend of it, and had booked them into a nearby hotel and ordered tickets for a theme park. The boys were very excited when they heard about this. Funny Folk Farm had the biggest and scariest rides of anywhere in Elfland! It would be good for Dwight as well, as he was spending too much time with his nose stuck in his laptop.

The visit to the Good Doctor went very well. Not only did he carry out all the tests on Tom in no time, but had the boys laughing from the moment they entered his room. The Good Doctor decided that Tom needed to use a very special computer program to help settle his right cherrycrawl hemipier, and was confident this would help, and all would be well.

The hotel was amazing! It had an indoor swimming pool in which the boys and Dwight could splash about, and a spa, where Ellie could be covered in mud. The boys thought that this was very strange; whenever they got covered in mud, they received a real telling off. "Typical", thought Tim, "when a grown-up gets covered in mud, it is good for the skin, but when a small boy does it, the same grown-up gets really angry".

The theme park was fantastic! The boys went on every ride that there was, mainly with their father, since their mother was something of a big girl's blouse when it came to really scary rides, though she did go on the Tea Cups twice. By the end of the day, the boys were exhausted, and after an early meal, bath and story, they were fast asleep in bed, and no doubt dreaming.

The following day, the whole family visited a park where you could walk with the animals. It was very exciting. Being up close to so many animals, and being able to touch some of them, was magical. There is something about interacting with animals that is very calming, and perhaps reminds us of our place in nature. Having washed their hands, everyone had an ice-cream, and went to the loo, before starting the long journey home.

The next day, Tom began his new computer treatment, and as he did so, started blinking. The blinking continued for a good twenty minutes, which caused his mother to email the Good Doctor in something of a panic. The Good Doctor reassured her that this was nothing to worry about; the blinking would fade once Tom's brain got used to the new stimulation, which might take a couple of weeks.

Sure enough, over the next two weeks, the blinking went away, and Tom returned to being the carefree boy he had been before. He would have to continue using the program for many weeks to come, and have to see the Good Doctor again, but for now, things were going really well.

Of a Saturday, Tom had started helping his father with the family business. He really enjoyed exporting Fairy Magic Marbles, which were now selling like hot cakes, but the whole business of buying-in all the strange foods was often beyond him. Try as he may, Tom could not believe anyone would want to eat a sardine that was not only full of mushy bones, but left your breath smelling like a whale's bottom.

During the family's next Skype consultation with the Good Doctor, Tom was brimming with confidence, and totally tic-free. The Good Doctor could not help but smile as he chatted to the young man, who now looked a picture of health. The Good Doctor told Tom all about a boy named Bard, who produced a monthly comic that always had a piece about children who struggled to read, or were a bit clumsy. He suggested that Tom should write something for the comic about what it is like to have tics.

Tom thought about it for a few days. He wasn't sure if he wanted to tell the world about his problems, but he eventually decided that he should. He talked to his mum about it, and then set about writing a piece for The Bard Comic. When it was finished, he put it in a big envelope and asked his dad if he had a large stamp. Fingers crossed.

When Bard, the Editor-in-Chief of The Bard Comic, received the big envelope with the equally big stamp, he was overjoyed. He had not read a piece about tics before, and this piece was really very well written. He immediately set about replying to Tom, and thanking him for the article, before getting his secretary to put it in the post without delay. (Bard's mother actually posted the letter, but it sounds better if you say "secretary").

When Tom's story appeared in the comic, both the Good Doctor and Miss Ariel Payne, who were regular readers, wrote to Tom to congratulate him on an excellent piece of work. They both said it took courage to tell the world about such things, and that they were sure it would be of great help to other children who have tics and are sad.

But it wasn't just grownups who were impressed with Tom's writing skills. Bard was so pleased with the feedback he received from other readers, he asked Tom to become a regular contributor. Tom even wrote a piece about how being worried can make you wet the bed, but changed the name of the child involved. He then wrote a whole range of articles about having a good diet, taking lots of exercise, and getting enough sleep.

In what Bard himself described as "a stroke of genius", Bard persuaded Tom to become the official sports writer for the comic, which meant Tom got to attend all the important fixtures of Bard United. At these games Tom met the giant Bradelf, who wasn't really a giant, as well as Gudhelf and Hob. Tom wrote some really good "copy", as they call it, and the boys became really great friends.

Tom learnt about the problems his new friends had gone through, and over a period of time, interviewed them, and others, which led to regular pieces in the comic. At the request of Bard, he even got to meet and interview the most famous girl gang in Elfland, the Sprite Girls, and had his picture taken with them. Wow!

The popularity of marbles continued to grow, and Dwight added more and more food items to his list of imports, even though Tom, who still found time to help him out in the office, could not imagine anyone would want to eat a gherkin, which he personally thought was no more than a very old, warty, pickled frog.

Ellie now had her quiet, relaxed husband back, and the boys were full of fun and enthusiasm for life. Old Flik, who would go on to live forever, would continue to plod around the garden, and occasionally find a reason to wag a finger at Ben. Every now and then, when Flikker saw the children playing in the garden without a care in the world, he would say to himself, "There, I told you, I'm no goat's bottom".

9 BOTTOM

On the 25th of June, which just so happened to be National Day in Slovenia (not that that had anything to do with what was about to unfold, other than that many folk in Elfland celebrate the day), a debacle of almost gargantuan proportions occurred. And that, let me tell you, is big.

For some weeks now, Tommy Ramsbottom had been blinking. More recently, he had even started grunting. Thinking that it might be the onset of Swine fever, Tommy's mother had taken him to the doctor, but Swine Fever was ruled out. In fact, the doctor suggested that Tommy might have a minor tic disorder that a lot of children have. According to the doctor, a tic disorder is so common, it is considered by some to be a "normal" phase of development.

Mrs Ramsbottom certainly did not want her son to have anything that was common, but was relieved to hear it was just a phase he was passing through. However, that relief came to an abrupt end at 10.32am on the 25th of June when, in the middle of Milly Elfin's general store and tearooms, Tommy blurted out, "Bottom". Following a moment's silence, there followed three more "bottoms", and another word that I will not mention, for fear of causing offence to those unaccustomed to such expletives.

The first rude word was all but ignored by the customers and staff of Mrs Elfin's emporium, who perhaps thought they had misheard the word. However, three "bottoms" in a row, and then the very rude word,(which, for the older reader, rhymes with "silly") was just too much, and caused a chain of events that would be described later in the Elftown Gazette as a "discombobulation" and "general hullabaloo", which tends to make you think it was very serious.

In fact, what happened was, this: in response to Tommy blurting out the said rude words, a rather large lady who might have been in some way

related to a troll, and who had been bending over selecting some large snails from a floured bucket for her tea, stood up and swung round. The act of swinging round so suddenly caused her wicker basket to swing out, and strike Mr Elfin. Until this point in time, Mr Elfin had been a tall, thin, upright man, but the force of the blow, and the region of contact, caused him to buckle in the middle and fall backwards.

Mr Elfin was fortunate that an open sack of flour broke his fall, but, unfortunately, the impact caused the sack to explode, and a cloud of smoke (actually flour) to fill the shop, and escape through open windows and doors into the street. Mr Elfin's cry of pain, and the shop and street filling with smoke (actually flour) caused customers and staff alike to scream, panic, and run in every direction.

This hullabaloo caused a horse to rear up, and then bolt down the street, two cars to swerve and crash, and a cyclist to lose his balance and strike a lamppost. While all this was happening, several people called the emergency services. Subsequently, seven police cars, two police motor cyclists, eight fire engines, and four ambulances arrived promptly at the scene.

Long before the dust (actually flour) had settled, and Sgt Trollop had assumed command of the situation, Mrs Ramsbottom had ushered Tommy away from the chaotic, floury scene. Not realising that it had been Tommy's rude words that had started this unfortunate chain of events, she had thought it best to remove him from the uproar, so as not to distress him any further! Oh dear. As she hurried and harried him along the street, and bustled him inside the family home, the number and variety of very rude words increased dramatically, and each rude word was accompanied by an array of very strange movements of his right arm, hand and fingers. Mrs Ramsbottom tried to comfort Tommy, then shouted at him. After a while, Tommy's mother did the only thing possible in this situation, and burst into tears.

When Albie A Ramsbottom returned home in response to his wife's frantic call, a weeping wife and a tear-soaked carpet confronted him. When he looked out of the window, out onto the garden, his heart sank, as he saw his son striding back and forth, shouting out very rude words, and waving his right arm in the air. He was about to run out into the garden and give Tommy a good telling off, but thought better of it and called the doctor instead.

The doctor said it sounded like a case of torn rats, but as he was not an expert on such matters, he would have to refer Tommy to a specialist, and would try to get an urgent appointment. Well, not only did they get an appointment for the following week, but the Good Doctor, as he was known, called Mrs Ramsbottom to reassure her, and provide her with directions for finding the clinic.

Due to the nature of poor Tommy's affliction, and the embarrassment that Mrs Ramsbottom, in particular, felt about the very rude words that now seemed to fill every waking moment, she had decided not to venture out, and keep Tommy at home, at least until he had seen the Good Doctor. This seemed to have a calming effect on Tommy, and by the time they had to travel to see the Good Doctor, the rude words were limited to the occasional, and almost whispered, B word.

On the long journey to the clinic, and indeed, during the long consultation, yet more and more rude words escaped from Tommy's lips, only now they were followed by a muffled "Sorry". The Good Doctor did not bat an eyelid as Tommy produced a tirade of bodily parts; he calmly went about the business of taking a detailed history from Mrs Ramsbottom, and testing Tommy. This done, he started explaining to Mr and Mrs Ramsbottom, but in particular, to Tommy, just what was happening, and more importantly, why.

When Tommy had started blinking, a group of very naughty goblins began teasing him. The teasing then turned to bullying, and the gang of goblins had thought it great fun to follow Tommy around, and steal his belongings from him. It seemed he could not escape from them, and, as the fear inside him grew, the blinking increased, and he started grimacing, snorting like a pig, and finally, saying rude words. The Good Doctor explained that saying rude words is not unusual, and is often triggered by seeing an object, like a large trolls bottom, or getting a word stuck in your head that keeps going round and round.

The Good Doctor made some changes to Tommy's diet, suggested some really good supplements to take, and told Tommy about a special computer game he wanted him to use each day to calm down the part of the brain that was causing the problem. However, he also said that the most important thing to do, was to remove the stress from his life, and that meant an entire gang of goblins. Surely no one could do that?

Once home, Mrs Ramsbottom tweaked Tommy's diet. She replaced his Coco Plops with a cooked breakfast, and she gave him Omegas 3 & 6 supplements, as well as zinc, magnesium and vitamins to take every day. She also made sure there was always fresh fruit in the fruit bowl, and, at lunch time, she prepared healthy sandwiches or a salad. In the evening, following the Good Doctor's advice, Tommy's mother cooked a totally scrumptious supper for the whole family.

Tommy did the computer treatment every day. But in the back of his mind was the thought that he would have to leave the comfort and safety of his home one day, and face the gang of goblins. No matter how hard he tried,

and no matter how brave he tried to be, the thought of seeing the gang again made him say rude words or have to rush to the loo. As far as Tommy was concerned, no matter how good the food was, no matter how brilliant the tablets and computer game were, nothing could defeat the gang of goblins, who, at some point in time, would try to get him again.

On Saturday the 26th of July, Albie Ramsbottom took Tommy for a kick-about at the local football club. The day had been organised by Bard Elf to provide an activity during the school holidays, but also, and I might say rather cunningly, to provide an opportunity to scout for potential new members of the club. This was the first time that Tommy had been out of the house since seeing the Good Doctor, but with his dad on the touchline, this seemed to be the ideal way to get back into the real world.

It would have been, but for the fact that his father needed to pop round the corner to the shops to pick up a couple of things Mrs Ramsbottom had forgotten, and Tommy needed to go to the toilets in the changing rooms. Having visited the loo and washed his hands, Tommy was heading back to the pitch when he spotted a goblin, then another one, then another one, and then the whole gang of goblins. He started sweating, his heart was thumping, and a string of rude words escaped from his lips, as slowly but surely, the gang closed in.

They started calling him names, told him he was dead meat, and then, in the greatest of detail, they told him how they were going to give him a really good thumping. Now when you are in a gang and you are calling people nasty names, you sometimes don't notice when an angry giant is approaching. Certainly, as the gang of goblins moved ever closer to the now trembling Tommy, they were totally unaware of the now extremely angry giant that was stood immediately behind them.

It was probably when the first two or three goblins literally took flight that the rest of the gang of goblins lost interest in bullying, as well as control of several bodily functions. Bradelf, the giant, had left the pitch when he too needed the loo, but as soon as he returned and saw what the goblins were doing, he became very angry. The giant Bradelf, who was not really a giant, but would have appeared so to the young goblins, did not like bullies, and his dislike of bullying was about to be pretty obvious to seventeen or so goblins.

If you can imagine a troll crossed with an ogre on a bad hair day, you will just begin to understand what the gang of goblins saw, just before they started flying off in every directions. Two goblins fainted before Bradelf had laid a hand on them, five started crying out of sheer terror, and all of them wet themselves either before, or while they were being flung high into the sky. By the time Bradelf had finished, goblins were scattered in all directions, and those who could, were running home to their mummies, crying like babies.

It was at this point that Bradelf turned to Tommy to see if he was OK. Tommy, just like the goblins, was convinced he was going to be eaten alive by a giant, and prepared himself for the event by fainting. When he came to, he was being carried back to the pitch in Bradelf's arms. As he opened his eyes and saw the giant's head just above his own, Tommy fainted again, as you would.

Bradelf handed Tommy over to the group of adults that were supervising the play day, and when Tommy regained consciousness for the second time, he saw the kindly faces of Mrs Elf and his father standing over him. He told them what had happened, about how the gang of goblins were going to beat him up, and how this giant had turned up from nowhere and attacked them, before coming to get him and probably eat him alive.

Mrs Elf could not help but laugh. Holding Tommy tight in her arms to reassure him, she called Bradelf over. As the giant (who wasn't really a giant) approached, Tommy was set to faint again, when Mrs Elf said, "This is Bradelf. He plays for our first team. It was he that saved you from the goblins. I don't think they will ever trouble you again. Not with a giant for a friend." And so it was.

Eighteen, to be precise, injured and rather smelly goblins hobbled home. They decided being in a gang and bullying elves is probably not a good idea, particularly when there are ogres on the loose in Elftown. Tommy joined the football team and became good friends with Bradelf (his hero), the Bard, Gudh, and Hob, to mention but a few. During his second season with the club he even managed to get a place in the first team.

Tommy stuck to his healthy diet, took his tablets every day, and did everything the Good Doctor asked him to do. As the weeks passed into months, all the funny little movements stopped as did the rude words, with the exception of the B word that he sometimes said to wind up his mother.

As Tommy was often seen in the company of Bradelf, not even the naughtiest of goblins ever considered bullying Tommy again. In fact, on seeing him walking down the street or crossing the playground, it was the goblins that would come over all unnecessary, start trembling, and feel an overwhelming desire to run away. Just remember, bullies are not brave and eventually end up suffering themselves.

10 LITTLE HARRY

Little Harry was very little. Not just because he was only four years old, but also because he was born a few weeks earlier than he should have been, even for an elf. As a consequence, he was rather small. He was very handsome, and a very good little boy really, but unfortunately, he was still in nappies, day and night, and could not speak. Although Harry could say a few words that only his mother understood, he never used sentences, or even put one word after another.

At playschool, he tended to play on his own, or stick close to the grown-ups. Mary Fairy, at nearly five years old, liked to mother him, and when Harry needed something, she spoke on his behalf. Apart from that, Harry amused himself in the sandpit, or just sat watching the other children as they played happily around him. His lack of speech meant he spent a lot of time alone in his own little world.

The grownups at the playschool were very good to Harry, making sure he was fed, and his water bottle was topped up, but apart from that, the grownups were not really sure what to do with him. He certainly showed no interest in learning numbers, or the elfabet, and to be honest, some of them wondered if perhaps he wasn't quite all there.

On Monday the 19th of May, Mary O'Rafferty, the Elfsted inspector, begun her annual visit to all the schools in Elftown, starting her day at the playschool attached to Elftown Primary School. It was there that she spotted Harry sitting alone in the sandpit, lost in his own little world. If there was one thing that Mary prided herself on, it was her knowledge of the little people, and clearly, here something was not right. She greeted him in her usual cheery Irish way, but received only a fleeting glance and a half smile in response.

Mary questioned the staff about the little boy in the sandpit, and seemed to want to know a great deal about him. In fact, she seemed to want to know more than the staff actually knew. By the time Mary's inspection was finished, Tilly Tully, who ran the school, had got in touch with the Special Needs Department at the main school, her friend Betty Button at the Department of Education, and as a consequence, Ellie Quence, the local Speech Therapist.

Meetings were arranged, assessments planned, and Harry's parents informed of what was happening following the visit of Mary O'Rafferty. Harry had already seen doctors at the hospital, but to date, nothing had been done to help him, and although his mother wished with all her heart that he would speak one day, secretly she feared that there was no hope. Many times after putting him to bed, when he had looked up at her and said, "Nigh", a tear had formed in her eye and rolled down her cheek.

On Saturday the 24th of May, Mrs Thistlebottom sat with her son, Harry, in Milly's tearooms enjoying a nice cup of tea, and a glass of milk. She had considered having scones and jam, but decided better of it, as the waistband of her skirt had felt a little tight that morning when getting dressed, and also Harry tended to react badly to sweet things. It was while these thoughts were going round in her head, that destiny came knocking. That is Des (short for Desdemona) Tinny, who accidentally bumped into Mrs Thistlebottom.

Having apologised profusely, Des asked if she might sit at their table, since the tea rooms were packed, and no other chair was available. Having sat down, Des did what all grownups do: she began chatting to Harry. When Harry did not respond, Des looked at Mrs Thistlebottom, who introduced herself, before explaining to her that Harry couldn't speak. Des listened to Violet as she talked at length about Harry, nodding her head as Violet explained everything.

When Violet eventually fell silent, Des said she knew a good bit about developmental delay, and had actually spent two weeks as an observer in a special clinic earlier that year.

Des was a gyro-tractor, or something like that, and was very interested in helping children with learning problems. Violet wanted to know everything there was to know about the clinic, and that meant a second pot of tea and a few biscuits, which surely would not have too many extra inches in them. As Des told Violet everything she had learnt at the clinic, her heart began to beat a little quicker, and an excitement she had not felt in ages welled up inside her.

The minute Violet got home, she cornered her husband and repeated everything Des had said about the clinic, explaining how the doctor there can helped children like Harry. Together, they looked on the internet and read every page of the clinic website. Violet was so excited that she bought and downloaded all of the Good Doctor's books, and with her husband, Ivor, wrote a very long email, which they sent to the clinic.

That evening, there was an air of excitement in the Thistlebottom household; and in the morning when they received a reply from the Good Doctor, you could have knocked Violet over with a feather. She was deliriously happy, and Ivor was beside himself, as they say (if that is possible). Not only had the Good Doctor replied to them on a Sunday, but he had offered them an appointment for Harry to be seen at the clinic in two weeks' time.

Ivor, probably due to a Scottish connection on his father's side, decided to take the caravan on the long journey to the clinic, and thus avoid the unnecessary expense of staying in a B&B. However, when telling Violet of his decision, he explained that he thought Harry would be happier in the caravan, than in some strange accommodation. Violet would have preferred a nice, comfortable hotel, but as it was, she was happy to agree.

The "tin snail", as Violet called the caravan when Ivor was out of earshot, made the long journey even longer, and Ivor had serious doubts about his little car and his beloved caravan being able to cross the mountains (actually downs) that lay between the family home and their destination in the New Forests of the Southlands. But arrive they did, albeit later than planned, and in a moment that Violet attributed to altitude sickness, Ivor

suggested that they visit a local inn rather than cook in the caravan. The following morning, they left the caravan site and headed off to meet the Good Doctor for Harry's appointment. The Good Doctor greeted them, and ushered them into his office. He chatted away to Harry, carefully observing his responses all the while. The Good Doctor gave Harry some crayons and paper before asking Mrs Thistlebottom what seemed like endless questions. With this done, he gave little Harry lots of tests, and a good few tickles, before explaining to Mr and Mrs Thistlebottom what he thought the problem was.

Not only had Harry been born much earlier than he should have been, even for an elf, but it had been a particularly long and difficult birth. The umbibumby cord had been wrapped around Harry's neck, and it had taken the midwife a little while to get him breathing normally. The Good Doctor explained that the stress of a difficult birth can cause the development of the brain to glitch, and this was why little Harry was not talking and growing as he should.

The Good Doctor gave Mrs Thistlebottom a lot of information about diet and supplements which he wanted Harry to have each day, and showed Mr Thistlebottom how to spin Harry on an office chair in an anticlockwise direction, and also how to assist Harry in doing exercises on the stairs. A Skype appointment was made for two months' time, and before they knew it, the family were in their little car heading for home.

The following day, Mrs Thistlebottom planned to put Harry on his new diet, arriving at the elfood shop at 9am. She bought the Vegepa Omega chewies, vitamins and minerals, and then hurried around the shops to get all the various foods the Good Doctor had suggested. This done, she took Harry to the park, and encouraged him to go on the swings, roundabout and slides, just like the Good Doctor had suggested. Harry had always been nervous of such activities, but today with his smiling mother by his side, he seemed to gain a new level of confidence.

At home, Mr Thistlebottom was cleaning and oiling an old office chair which had been relegated to the garden shed long ago. Although he had listened carefully to what the Good Doctor had said about the need to stimulate Harry's cherrybellbum, he really could not see how spinning Harry anticlockwise was going to help. However, as Mr Thistlebottom knew, to his cost, it was not wise to cross his wife when she was on a mission, and today was one of those days.

By the time Violet and Harry returned from the park, the chair, now looking like new, was positioned in the middle of the sitting room, ready for action. Mr Thistlebottom placed Harry on the chair and rotated him slowly three times anticlockwise. He then said, "Boo" to get Harry's attention and looked

MORE

at his eyes. As they were perfectly still, he repeated the whole process twice more.

Harry seemed to love being spun, and as his father stopped the last of the nine rotations, Harry looked up at his father and said, "More! More!" This time it was Mr Thistlebottom who could have been knocked over with a feather. It was as if the spinning had thrown a switch in Harry's brain. Harry seemed to be much more engaged, and to want more stimulation.

Over the next few weeks, Harry started saying more and more words, and on more than one occasion, he said, "Wee-wee", which of course is Elfish tongue for "Mother, I need the toilet". When his daddy left for work, Harry would now say "Bye-bye, Daddy," often quickly followed by "Me go park". Mrs Thistlebottom could not believe what was happening, but with every new word, her heart bounced with joy, and she could not wait for their next talk with the Good Doctor, and the next treatment to be put in place.

On the day of the planned Skype with the Good Doctor, Mrs Thistlebottom did her hair, put on her make-up with extra care, and spent an age deciding what to wear. In Elfland, everybody, with perhaps the exception of younger goblins and, of course, the Northern Trolls, believed in the old ways, which included respecting their elders and professionals, like the Good Doctor.

Having insisted that Ivor put on a tie, and having brushed Harry's hair at least three times, they all sat down in front of the computer in readiness for the Skype consultation with the Good Doctor. Fortunately, the internet was at full strength, and it could not have gone better. The Good Doctor asked about the diet, supplements and exercises, before asking about what progress had been made.

Mrs Thistlebottom started talking about Harry's speech and toilet training. It's likely she would still be talking now, if it were not for Harry saying a string of words, which caused the Good Doctor to start laughing, and fortunately interrupt Mrs Thistlebottom's flow. As Mrs Thistlebottom paused to draw breath, the Good Doctor outlined what was needed to be done next, and then scheduled their next appointment at the clinic in the New Forests of the Southlands for two months time.

This time, at Mrs Thistlebottom's insistence, the tin snail was left at home, and a reservation made for a room at the local hostelry with an en suite bathroom. Needless to say, the journey took half the time without the tin snail, and before they knew it they were dining in style, albeit surrounded by turf cutters which abound in these parts.

The second assessment at the clinic could not have gone better, and the Good Doctor was over the moon at the progress little Harry was making. His speech was coming on in leaps and bounds, and by day he was largely dry and no longer needing a nappy. Now, even at night, he was sometimes dry, and Mr Thistlebottom (with the Scottish connection on his father's side) had noticed how the housekeeping money was stretching further.

With new treatments in place, and progress gathering pace with every new day, it was soon time for Harry to have his first day at Elftown Primary School. Following Mary O'Rafferty's visit to Harry's playschool, every resource possible had been put in place in readiness for Harry's first day at "big boys' school", as his mother had called it.

SENCOs, a Speech Therapist, and an Educated Psychologist were all on hand for when not-so-little Harry arrived for his first day at Elfton Primary School. Ellie Quence carried out a SALT assessment, which has nothing to do with pepper and the like, but rather, involved overseeing tests all about speaking. Ellie arranged for Harry to have speech therapy in school each day. Miss Spelling, who was in charge of the Special Needs Department, and a graduate of the University of Reading, also arranged all sorts of assessments, including a meeting with Ed Sykes, the Educated Psychologist.

Everybody at the school was overjoyed with the outcome of all the assessments. Following a very long meeting where people nodded when not speaking, and during which, a great deal of tea was sipped and countless biscuits eaten, a plan was put in place to help Harry to catch up with his speech and learning. Mary Fairy helped too: she appointed herself as little Harry's shadow, making sure he was alright, and that no one picked on him. Two very naughty goblins, who had teased Harry, found themselves with what could have been hopeless hiccups, had it not been for Mary reversing

the spell she had put on them after an hour.

Days passed into weeks, and the terms flew by. There were more Skype conversations with the Good Doctor, and a couple of visits to the clinic. Each time the Good Doctor and Harry's parents chatted, the Good Doctor was delighted with little Harry's progress. More and more treatments were put in place to help Harry to read and write easily, and before you could say, "Well, I'll be a goat's bottom!" he was holding his own in class.

The school had thought about holding Harry back for a year, but following another long meeting involving all the people that were helping Harry, which, of course, involved nodding when not speaking, sipping tea and eating endless biscuits, it was decided that he should not be held back. This was probably just as well, as Mary Fairy would not have been happy about this, and, as a result, all the people involved might have ended up with terminal trumping as a consequence.

Mary Fairy was an avid reader of the Bard Comic. One day, Mary suggested to little Harry that they should write a story all about what it was like when he couldn't speak, and how, with all the help he had received, he was now able to talk the hind legs off a donkey, but also read, write and do his sums. Mary helped Harry with the writing, and Harry produced an absolutely brilliant series of little drawings to illustrate the story.

When it was completed, Mary cast a little spell over it to make sure all the spellings were correct, and then posted it off to the Editor-in-Chief of the Bard Comic. Bard received quite a few stories in the post, but this one, with its beautiful illustrations really touched him. If he hadn't been a hardnosed editor and the manager of a top class football team, he would have shed a little tear.

The Editor-in-Chief wrote back to Mary and Harry, telling them how much he had enjoyed their story, as well as Harry's brilliant illustrations, and he said that it would be included in the next edition of the comic.

When the story was published, it was not just Mr and Mrs Thistlebottom that wept a tear or two, but endless parents and teachers who had been touched by the sadness, and eventual triumph of one little boy.

In the fullness of time, Harry would excel at school, become an excellent sportsman, and one day play for Elftown United. He would even score a magnificent goal, which people would talk about endlessly, especially after they had spent too long in the pub! Who would have thought that the little boy sat alone in the sandpit would one day be a sporting legend, and a graduate of the University of Reading?

ELFLAND INFORMATION

Country: Elfland

Capital city: Port Elf

Major towns: Wizardton, Elfton, Ashton, Old Port (Isle of Widget)

Small towns: Spritely Minster, Windy Bottom, Tiddleton, East Tiddleton, Tiddleton-on-Sea, West End, East End, Trumpington, Much Trumping-on-the-Marsh, Brook (Isle of Widget), Ventnoir (Isle of Widget), Seaview Sands (Isle of Widget), Reekin, Winkleton

Districts: Elfex, Northlands, Far Northlands, Southlands, Gobham County, Eastlands, Westlands, Isle of Widget (see official map)

Areas: Sandy Bottom (a popular skinny-dipping spot among goblins)

Rivers: The Tiddle, The Piddle, The Sidhe

Shops, tearooms, restaurants and pubs: Milly Elfin's General Store and Tearooms, Elfton. Proprietor Milly Elfin. Husband Mr Elfin. McDonkey's, The

Tiddly Trumper (Much-Trumping-on-the-Marsh), The Boar's Head(Westend), Winkle Inn(Winkleton), The Turf Cutter's Arms (Tiddleton-on-Sea)

Hospitals: Great Orcmond Street Hospital, Port Elf

Clinic: Tiddly House, Tiddleton, New Forests of the Southlands

Newspaper: Elfton Gazette

Theme parks: Fairy Down Meadow Adventure Park (near Wizardton), Funny Folk Farm Theme Park (near Tiddly House Clinic, in the Southlands)

Stately homes: Orcborne House and Beau Lieu, Isle of Widget

Film studios: Folly Wood

Schools: Wizardton Primary School (Bard's school), Wizardton East Primary School (Gudh's school), Elfton Primary School, Brook Primary School, Old Port Primary School, Port Elf West Primary School, Wallopham School for Boys, Westend Primary School and Playschool

Forests: New Forests of the Southlands, Forests of the Northlands

Football teams: Elfield United, Ashton Villa, Elfton United (Badh's team), National team Elfland

Principal Characters

Badh Elf (A.k.a. The Bard)
Mother/Father: Mrs & Mr W Elf
Siblings: None
Address: Gremlin Close, Wizardton
School attended: Wizardton Primary School

Gudh Elf
Mother/Father: Mrs & Mr H Elf
Father's occupation: Vet
Siblings: Sister
Address: Fairy Tale, Crescent, Wizardton

Bradelf (the giant)
Mother/Father:Mr & Mrs Elf
Father's occupation:Builder
Siblings:None
Address:3 Wizards Way, Wizardton
School attended: Wizardton Primary School

Hob Goblin
Mother/father:Rob (Roberta)/Bob
School attended:Special School, Wizardton.

Hob Nob (A.k.a.Ugli)
Mother/father: Mrs & Mr Nob
Father's occupation: Land owner

Address: Noblis Hall, Wizardton
Siblings: None

Humphrey Boggart*
*Boggart: the child of an elf and a fairy
Nicknames: Bogey/Boogie
Mother/father: Honeybee &Hardley
Siblings: None
Address: Casablanca, 16 De Forest Drive, Wizardton
School attended: Wizardton Primary School

Tom Tickler
Mother/father: Ellie &Dwight
Siblings: Tim
Address: Manor Farm, Gnomemansland
School attended: Elfton Primary School

Tommy Ramsbottom
Mother/father: Prudence & Albie A Ramsbottom
Siblings: None
Address: Elfton
School attended: Elfton Primary School

Harry Thistlebottom (A.k.a. Little Harry)
Mother/father: Violet & Ivor Thistlebottom
Siblings: None
Address: Elfton
School attended: Elfton Primary School and Playschool

Teaching Staff

Wizardton Primary School

Mr Whackham: Headmaster of Wizardton Primary School when Bard was Badh. Now retired

Mrs Longbottom: Schoolteacher at Badh's school (Wizardton Primary School), and wife of Avery

Miss Ariel Payne: Special Needs teacher at Badh's school

Ms Bee Stake: Teacher at Wizardton Primary School. Engaged to Elphin Tiddly

Mrs Sidebottom: Wizardton Primary School Headmistress following Mr Whackham's retirement

Miss Fortune: Lily Pari's form teacher

Trixie Pixie: Classroom assistant (BSc Spritecology)

Miss Spelling: Head of special needs at Wizardton Primary School, and a graduate of Reading University

Other Professional Characters:

Mary O'Rafferty: The Elfsted inspector
Tilly Tully: Playschool head
Betty Button: Department of Education representative
Ellie Quence: Speech Therapist
Ed Sykes: Educated Psychologist
The Good Doctor: Tiddly House Clinic, The New Forests of the Southlands

More Characters

Grownups

Avery Longbottom: Mrs Longbottom's husband
Des ("Desdemona") Tinny: Gyro-tractor
Sgt. Trollop: Elfton police officer
Sid Sidebottom: Chauffeur at Noblis Hall
Flikker Urist: Head gardener at Manor Farm. Also known as "Old Flik"
Ben Doone: Under gardener at Manor Farm

Children

Randelf: Badh's friend and classmate
The Sprite Girls: Hairy Mary, Smelly Ellie, Sweaty Betty, Silly Lily (Lil the Brill/Lily Pari), Smiley Kylie
Eddie Ramsbottom: Also known as Little Willy
Fate: The sister of a Bard United player
Lollilou & Freya Winterbottom: Fairies
Mary Fairy: Friend of Harry Thistlebottom

Types of Character

Elves

Goblins

Fairies

Boggarts

Bogles

Trolls

Ogres

Orcs

Green Orcs

Neurological Terms/Disorders

Cherrybellbum

Cherry crawl hemi pier

Thrummy Cap syndrome

Trollism

Ogreism

Terminal Trumping

A Diction

Gun-cushion

Collywobbles

Abominable My-grain

For further information, please visit www.tinsleyhouseclinic.co.uk

The Official Colouring Book

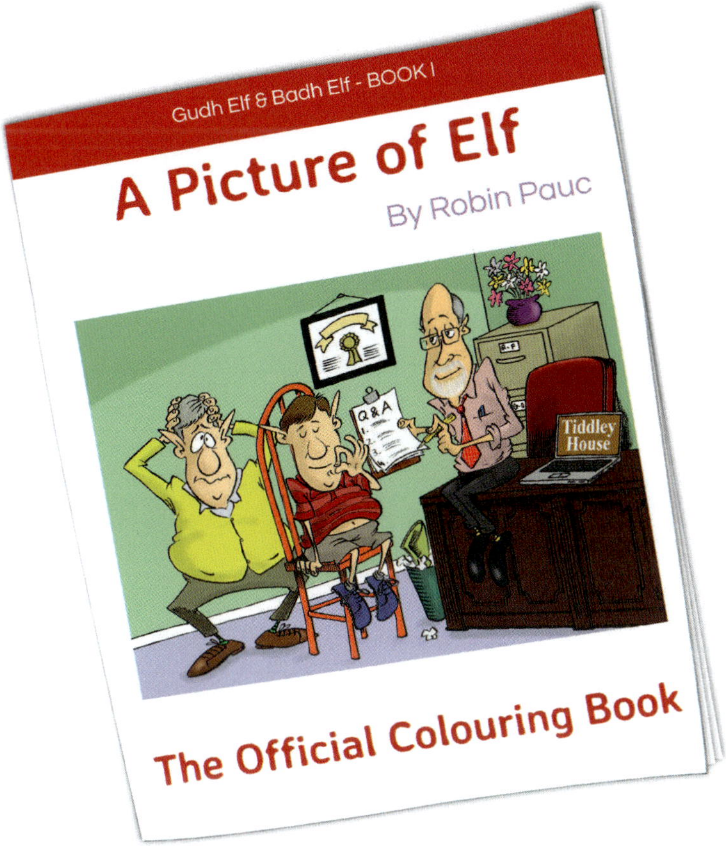

Des Campbell - illustrator extraordinaire

Gudh Elf & Badh Elf - Book I A Picture of Elf - The Official Colouring Book

Use the amazing illustrations by Des in A Picture of Elf to help you colour in the pictures.

AVAILABLE NOW

11818930R10084

Printed in Great Britain
by Amazon.co.uk, Ltd.,
Marston Gate.